SOME SAID IT THUNDERED

OLIVER
NELSON

BY THE SAME AUTHOR:

Come Holy Spirit
Does God Speak Today?

CONTRIBUTIONS TO:

Michael Harper, *Bishop's Move*
Kevin Springer (ed.), *Riding the Third Wave*
Jill Dobson and David Lonsdale, *Can Spirituality Be Taught?*

Foreword by Dr. John White

SOME
SAID IT
THUNDERED

A Personal Encounter with the Kansas City Prophets

Afterword by Jamie Buckingham

DAVID PYTCHES

A Division of
Thomas Nelson Publishers
Nashville

Published in Nashville, Tennessee, by Oliver-Nelson Books, a division of Thomas Nelson, Inc., Publishers, and distributed in Canada by Lawson Falle, Ltd., Cambridge, Ontario. First published in Great Britain by Hodder and Stoughton.

Unless otherwise noted, the Bible version used in this publication is THE NEW KING JAMES VERSION. Copyright © 1979, 1980, 1982, Thomas Nelson, Inc., Publishers.

Scripture quotations noted KJV are from The King James Version of the Holy Bible.

Printed in the United States of America.

ISBN 0-8407-9128-3

1   2   3   4   5   6—96   95   94   93   92   91

To my dear friend Barry Kissell, whom I inherited as a colleague, since he had already been on the staff of St Andrew's Church, Chorleywood, for many years.

His faithfulness to God and boldness in stepping out for Him has evoked my unwavering admiration as he has ministered both at home and abroad in the power of the Holy Spirit. His unique gift for communicating the Word of God in such original and relevant ways has often refreshed and stimulated my understanding of the kingdom of God and the Gospel of Jesus Christ. His gentle and creative gift in leading the body of Christ into the presence of God in worship has enhanced some of the richest spiritual experiences of my life. His humble listening and loving counsel to individual clergy and laity alike have been an example to observe with awe and to model with delight.

These qualities, together with our almost daily fellowship in prayer, his outrageous sense of fun, and loyal friendship in the service of Christ, have made our twelve years of working together some of the most memorable and worthwhile in my life. Thanks be to God!

CONTENTS

FOREWORD

I suppose it was inevitable that it should happen. Any outstanding work of God (any outstanding work that even *purports* to be of God) sooner or later pulls a storm of controversy about its ears. The famous Kansas City prophets are now the center of such a storm. Or, to change the metaphor, the lines are drawn and a battle has begun.

It began when a Christian leader prepared a tape discussing the prophets in a derogatory manner. He also had his staff compile a 250-page document (dignified with the appellation "research") that was designed to discredit and ridicule them. He circulated the material to Christian leaders over North America. At least one Christian television program gave the matter extensive coverage. Now the controversy is spreading more widely yet, crossing the Atlantic.

The Battle Behind the Battle

Battles about prophets have plagued the church from time to time. Early last century it was the Irvingite controversy in London, with the leading prophet having to confess after years that he had been deceived. Many of us have found that hearing from

God is no easy thing. In fact, the Church has had so many bad experiences with prophets that now we react too rapidly and fearfully. We could be in danger of discarding a live baby in our horror over dirty bath water.

Most Christian rows major in bruised egos, exaggerations and fictions (many of them rumor-based), and inadequately researched charges. Careful investigations in Kansas since the charges suggest that such looks like the case there.

Yet I believe that for historical reasons, this battle will be different—fiercer, more bitter. It may well be a repeat of the battles surrounding Moses (the first prophet) and Jesus (the ultimate, though not the last, prophet). Biblical prophets display two characteristics: they speak the word of God, and frequently they perform miraculous signs confirming the truth of their word. In Moses and in Jesus the world saw that combination. Both performed miracles and spoke powerful words from God.

False prophets present themselves similarly—with miraculous signs and words. They challenged Moses in Egypt. The priests who conveyed the will of the gods to Pharaoh showed that they, too, could turn rods into serpents, could turn water into blood, could conjure frogs from the Nile. But God's power was greater. The day came when Pharaoh's priests said of Moses' signs, "This is none other than the finger of God." They knew they faced the only real source of power and wisdom, the power and wisdom no satanic arts could stand against.

If I am correct, the controversy that will threaten to divide the church during the nineties will therefore be of unusual ferocity. The nineties may see prophetic action reestablished. It will be important to know who are the true, and who are the false, prophets. We may actually live through the final phase of the battle over miraculous power in today's church.

What do the time of Moses, the time of Jesus, and the present time have in common? Remember, Satan does not seem to know

God's plans, but he seems to smell when something is afoot. All three periods are periods of major Satan-inspired infanticide. The first was more than Pharaoh's idea to avoid a revolt. It was Satan's attempt to prevent the arrival of a Moses on the earthly scene. The second period saw his attempt to prevent the earthly coming of the King of kings. And now? Well, has there ever in world history been so worldwide and systematic an attempt to kill infants? Why? Is it Satan's attempt to anticipate what God may be doing, and prevent it?

If there is anything that Satan dreads, it is the divine word. Always he will do his utmost to discredit it. The first Word came to Adam, "but of the tree . . . you shall not eat, for in the day that you eat of it you shall surely die" (Gen. 2:17).

Satan quickly tried to sow doubt in Eve's mind. Eve's doubts eventually ushered in the Fall and the rule of Satan.

> So when the woman saw that the tree was good for food, that it was pleasant to the eyes, and a tree desirable to make one wise, she took of its fruit and ate. She also gave to her husband with her, and he ate. . . . Then to Adam He said, "Because you have heeded the voice of your wife, and have eaten from the tree of which I commanded you, saying, 'You shall not eat of it': Cursed is the ground for your sake; in toil you shall eat of it all the days of your life" (Gen. 3:6, 17).

Again, when the Son of man came on the planet and heard the devastating word of God at his baptism, telling him in effect who he was, and why he was on earth, the devil came and said, "If You are the Son of God, command this stone to become bread" (Luke 4:3). Each of the three temptations recorded carries the same implication: "Did God really speak to you? Or did you just imagine it?"

Satan fears those words that come fresh from God's lips. He has been effective in neutralizing the written Word, by rendering it feeble as it drips from the lips of preachers who only believe it in their heads, but fail to experience its power in their lives. From such lips the Word carries little power. Because Satan so dreads the fresh Word, he will arouse controversy wherever it comes forth miraculously through the lips of a real prophet or from the lips of an evangelist aflame with the Spirit.

Contemporary prophets do not add to biblical revelation. Their mission is to give emergency instructions in battle, to bring the contemporary emphasis. They make revelation come alive again, authenticating and making vivid in the twentieth century the accounts of prophetic action in the Scripture.

War Between the Saints

It is tragic that war should so characterize the Christian body. Controversy according to the nineteenth century's Henry Venn should never be a matter of name calling. Venn urged us never to name names. We should focus, he said, on understanding the error (if there is one) and on explaining the difference between truth and error. Our battles would prove far less acrimonious if we followed his advice.

Yet before we look at the Kansas controversy more carefully, let us remind ourselves of a few facts. First, let us look at ways of distinguishing prophets false and true. Then let us see what kind of men some biblical prophets were. Let us give ourselves biblical orientation.

Beware of False Prophets

Beware of false prophets, who come to you in sheep's clothing, but inwardly they are ravenous wolves (Matt. 7:15).

Then many false prophets will rise up and deceive many (Matt. 24:11).

> For false christs and false prophets will rise and show signs and wonders to deceive, if possible, even the elect (Mark 13:22).

We are warned that it is to happen. Most scholars feel the words of Jesus apply particularly to the last days. They may be approaching us now. How are we to discern the false from the true? For one thing, *true prophets will be unpopular*.

> Woe to you when all men speak well of you, for so did their fathers to the false prophets (Luke 6:26).

One point in favor of the Kansas City prophets is that early in their ministry a storm of controversy has burst around them. Most prophets came to sticky ends. Jesus was attacked; though crowds followed him gladly, he was popular only for a time. Increasing opposition came against him from among God's people and, curiously, from adherents to Scripture and trained experts in Scripture—the Pharisees and doctors of the law. Theological degrees, valuable as they may be, do not guarantee spiritual discernment.

Unpopularity and rejection from among the people of God can hardly be the only criterion of true prophets. Moses sought to instruct God's people about false ones. The message was severe, but plain. *True prophets promote obedience to God*.

> "But the prophet who presumes to speak a word in My name, which I have not commanded him to speak, or who speaks in the name of other gods, that prophet shall die." . . . when a prophet speaks in the name of the LORD, if the thing does not happen or come to pass, that is the thing which the LORD has not spoken; the prophet has spoken it presumptuously; you shall not be afraid of him (Deut. 18:20, 22).

Curiously, the only prophet put to death in Scripture was Jesus. No other prophet is so treated by man. Jeremiah seems to interpret Moses' words differently from the way we do. In the middle of an impassioned discussion of the matter, God himself makes it clear that *he* will be responsible to deal with false claims to speak his word.

And as for the prophet and the priest and the people who say, "The oracle of the LORD!" I will even punish that man and his house (Jer. 23:34).

Anyone who has experience in helping to nurture "baby prophets" realizes that they have difficulty in distinguishing the words that the Spirit speaks from those that come from their own hearts or even from evil sources. At first they make many mistakes. We know they hear from God because of the reality of the true words they speak. I suppose the biblical "schools of the prophets" dealt with this kind of problem.

Authentic Dollar Bills

The United States Treasury once taught people how to distinguish counterfeit dollar bills without allowing them ever to see one. They argued correctly that to know the false it is only necessary— but *very* necessary—to know the true well. So the workers spent their time examining genuine money. They were not allowed to look at counterfeits. Clearly, in the same way, the best way to recognize false prophets will be to have close acquaintance with genuine prophets.

Unfortunately, not many of us have friends who hold recognized prophetic office. I believe there are very few around the world. The Scripture has, however, given us a sort of description to help us. John addresses the question in his first epistle:

Beloved, do not believe every spirit, but test the spirits, whether they are of God; because many false prophets have gone out into the world. By this you know the Spirit of God: Every spirit that confesses that Jesus Christ has come in the flesh is of God (1 John 4:1, 2).

Many people take John's word *spirit* to mean "demon." This is a mistaken idea. In any case, demons lie. Some do confess that he has come. They did so in Jesus' day and they do so now.

"Let us alone! What have we to do with You, Jesus of Nazareth? Did You come to destroy us? I know You, who You are—the Holy One of God!" But Jesus rebuked him, saying, "Be quiet, and come out of him!" And when the demon had thrown him in their midst, it came out of him and did not hurt him. . . . And demons also came out of many, crying out and saying, "You are the Christ, the Son of God!" And He, rebuking them, did not allow them to speak, for they knew that He was the Christ (Luke 4:34, 35, 41).

John's concern is with human spirits, especially those of false prophets, and the "spirit" behind their prophesying and teaching. It will be a teaching in which not only the divinity, but also *the full humanity* of Jesus is confessed. It must include the full acceptance of the virgin birth, the real death, and the physical resurrection from the dead, in a body which though in one sense "spiritual" (able to inhabit eternity) still had physical properties— like the ability to eat. Jonathan Edwards, perhaps the greatest biblical thinker of the past three centuries, sees the whole chapter as dealing with false and true prophets.

The true prophet's spirit will be one that overcomes worldliness—"the lust of the flesh, the lust of the eyes, and the pride" (1 John 2:15, 16). I would say, from my acquaintance with the Kansas City prophets, that they rate high here. No charges of sexual misconduct, acquisitiveness, or arrogance can truly be laid at their doors.

A real prophet *awakens in his hearers a greater confidence in biblical (or godly) truth.* This is what John means when he says:

We are of God. He who knows God hears us; he who is not of God does not hear us. By this we know the spirit of truth and the spirit of error (1 John 4:6).

This is, of course, a description of discernment—spiritual discernment as opposed to discernment by rule of biblical exegesis. Yet from the verses that follow it is clear that a real prophet's influence promotes godly love. Almost all of the remaining verses in 1 John 4 reveal a further characteristic of true prophets. Their influence promotes true love—to God, to brothers and sisters in Christ, to their neighbors, to heathens, to people everywhere. Their love will have the same qualities as Christ's.

Beloved, if God so loved us, we also ought to love one another. No one has seen God at any time. If we love one another, God abides in us, and His love has been perfected in us (1 John 4:11, 12).

Prophets are, of course, human beings. *As such, they can make mistakes and lie.* They need not cease to be prophets for their mistakes and failings, as a biblical account of two prophets demonstrates clearly.

Glory and Tragedy in the Life of a Prophet

Their stories are told in two astonishing passages of Scripture— 1 Kings 13 and 2 Kings 23. The glory of the stories resides in the magnificent boldness of one prophet, the miraculous and dramatic sign that accompanies his prophecy, and its astonishing fulfillment two and a half centuries later. Its tragedy lies in the needless death of that prophet.

In the story, a young prophet from Judah does something which from a human point of view would appear the height of foolhardiness. He turns up just as Jeroboam, first king of Israel, is about to offer a sacrifice on a new altar. The prophet cries out against the altar. He prophesies that a future Judean king would burn the bones of godless priests on the same altar. He actually names the king—Josiah. The record of the fulfillment of that prophecy occurs in 2 Kings 23:16—nearly three centuries later.

> As Josiah turned, he saw the tombs that were there on the mountain. And he sent and took the bones out of the tombs and burned them on the altar, and defiled it according to the word of the LORD which the man of God proclaimed, who proclaimed these words.

The sign that confirms the prophecy guarantees its truth. He declares that the altar is about to be split apart and its ashes poured out.

A word from God sometimes comes to me. Often I am terrified by the content of that word. "Is that really you, Lord? Please, please confirm what you said—if it *is* you." More than once, not from rebellion so much as from sheer terror, I have cried out, "No Lord! Never! No way!"

Prophets need "guts." The prophet in 1 Kings 13 runs two kinds of risk, that the sign will not take place and that a foreign king will kill him even if it does. Sometimes God has given me a deep assurance of what will happen. But at other times I have had to obey while still terrified. If you should say, "But the altar had to split, he spoke the word of the Lord!" your theology is correct. But, correct or not, you might feel differently if you had to do it yourself. A prophet's role is tough.

Jeroboam reacts quickly, ordering that the prophet be seized. But as he points to him, his arm withers and is paralyzed. He stands before the ruined altar, finding he has to beg the man of God to intercede for him. Once he is healed he invites his adversary to dinner.

The prophet refuses the invitation. God has instructed him to return home by another route and to eat nothing. However, as he returns, an older prophet meets him and tells him, as the young prophet protests, that the Lord's instructions have changed. He, too, invites him to dine. But the older prophet is lying.

> "I too am a prophet as you are, and an angel spoke to me by the word of the LORD, saying, 'Bring him back with you to your house, that he may eat bread and drink water.' " But he lied to him (1 Kings 13:18).

At this point mystery and awe haunt the story. As the two are dining, God's word comes to the older prophet, who is impelled by God himself to announce his younger colleague's death.

> Now it happened, as they sat at the table, that the word of the LORD came to the prophet who had brought him back; and he cried out to the man of God who came from Judah, saying, "Thus says the LORD: 'Because you have disobeyed the word of the Lord, and have not kept the commandment which the LORD your God commanded you, but you came back, ate bread, and drank water in the place of which the LORD said to you, "Eat no bread and drink no water," your corpse shall not come to the tomb of your fathers' " (1 Kings 13:20–22).

Probably crushed by guilt at the results of his deception, the old prophet saddles a donkey for the younger man before sending him on his way. On the journey, a lion kills him. The donkey and the lion wait quietly beside the body, until the old prophet returns to take it and bury it. The old man is obviously deeply repentant. Nevertheless, *and even before the repentance occurred,* the word of the Lord still came to him.

The Frail Humanity of True Prophets

How can we summarize the lessons that the passage teaches us?

1. Prophets can make serious mistakes. Presumably there are

aspects of prophetic experience that call for training—hence prophetic schools.

2. True prophets can lie and be manipulative in just the same way as false prophets.

3. The word of the Lord may still come to the prophet even though he has sinned. The appointment to prophetic office seems to be "without repentance."

But there is a lesson for us all here. God desires to speak to us individually. When a prophet professes to give us a "word" we must not accept it automatically, but bring it before the Lord ourselves. Certainly, if the greatest prophet in the world should meet me and tell me, "I've seen an angel. God has changed his mind about what he told you," I must not accept the authenticity of that word. The young prophet should have done this. *Never forget that a true prophet can bring a false word that purports to be from the Lord.* It is a grave offense, but it has occurred.

God is very serious about his word. It is not that he delights in punishment. He realizes that he must teach us to respect it if we are to take part in his deliverance of us all. And it will be so increasingly during the nineties as more prophets, with gifts like the prophets of old, are raised up.

The Kansas City Prophets

Like the two prophets in 1 Kings 13, and like all prophets in all times, the Kansas City prophets are human beings. They can make, and sometimes have made, mistakes. But they are true prophets. I know that, for I have observed them personally, and I have been at the receiving end of prophetic statements that came from God. Moreover, they were of another order than what passes for prophecy these days.

John Wimber had been troubled about two of them—not about

the reality of their calling, nor yet about their moral standing—
for about twelve months before the criticism arose. Many of
the statements in the criticism seem to be either untrue or un-
founded.

The Christian public tends to treat a real prophet rather like
a cross between a guru and a fortune teller. The prophets were
besieged with people who wanted "a word from God." Sometimes they seemed to feel that such remarkable people must
know everything there was to know. These believers assumed
that the prophets' capacity to hear from God would automatically
be accompanied by a profound grasp of theology—which not
all prophets have. Under the pressures of public exposure, two
of them not only spoke forth words of revelation, but sometimes
also gave their opinion about theological questions. Neither had
an adequate grasp of theology. While they never passed these
opinions off as words from the Lord, some people who listened
accepted their private opinions on the same level as revelation.

I must emphasize that only two of the prophets were involved.
They have since been temporarily "censored" by John Wimber.
Wimber had been concerned for a year about the problem, but
was in no position to do anything other than pass an opinion.

Recently two things permitted, even impelled, him to act.
One was that the Kansas City Fellowship placed itself under
the wing of Vineyard. The other was that the controversy broke
out almost at once. Wimber was in Australia at the time, so he
was forced to deal with the matter quickly. One of the men
expressed sorrow, realizing the nature of his error. The other
(who also regretted what happened) will spend considerable time
receiving a more thorough biblical grounding from a competent
and recognized Bible scholar.

Prophets are people, people with "passions and parts" like
the rest of us. God loves them just as he loves us. But because
they must convey his immediate words to others, he will be

more severe with them. He does not love them less, but he knows the terrible consequences to his people of false messages. (In Scripture God was so concerned about the matter of prophecy that he also severely punished his people for their dealings with the prophets.)

As we approach an age where preliminary indications may at last give way to end times (they had to come some time!) let us approach problems with cool heads, charitable hearts, and a broad knowledge of the Word of God.

Supplementary Information

The critic's charges had two sides to them, one concerning alleged false prophecies, the other concerning Pastor Mike Bickle's alleged wrongdoing in "taking over" churches on the basis of prophecies.

A thorough and careful investigation was conducted mostly by Dr. Jack Deere, formerly of Dallas Theological Seminary, currently of the Vineyard Christian Fellowship. He found that in fact no prophet was involved in any so-called takeover. Many churches had requested association with Bickle's church (Kansas City Fellowship). Most of these were not granted formal association, and in all cases very careful consideration was given to the requests. In one case a prophet reported, subsequent to the association, that he had "heard from the Lord" that it would take place. He made the announcement *after* the association had been decided on, having no knowledge that negotiations were underway. Charges also of bad financial dealings proved to be false and based on malicious documentation.

Two supposedly false prophecies could hardly be so called. Both concerned the *reporting* of prophetic fulfillment, years after both the prophecies had been fulfilled. Both were prophecies by Bob Jones. In one there was exaggeration. Bob had predicted that God would take the lives of a certain number of people in a certain church if they failed to forsake their sin. Over the years the number had grown in his mind from five to seven. The present pastor of the church subsequently admitted to Jack Deere that five unexpected deaths had taken place, two of them violent deaths.

The other prophecy concerned a drought predicted to begin on "the last day of June, or the first day of July." There were a number of precise details to the prophecy, every one of which was accurate. Long after the prophecy had been fulfilled, Pastor Bickle reported it publicly. In doing so he was uncertain whether the drought had been predicted for the beginning or the end of June, and made the wrong guess. The U.S. weather records for the dates actually predicted reveal that the drought was the second worst drought in 100 years. Clearly it is important to report accurately, and the Kansas City Fellowship acknowledges this. However, the charge of false prophecies is itself false.

A third report of an alleged false prophecy had more unfortunate consequences to grieving parents bereaved of a young child. They had delayed taking the child to the hospital, misjudging the urgency of the sickness. Efforts by the hospital staff to save the child's life were unsuccessful. However, there had been no prophecies involved, false or otherwise. The report had no factual basis, nor could its authors document any. The parents were astonished and shocked by the report, which appears to have been based on gossip and rumor. The accusation caused the parents great distress, and reawakened their sense of failure in not getting the child to the hospital earlier.

Finally, certain accusations about Paul Cain proved to be entirely false, having been based on untruths that were later acknowledged as such. Paul Cain met with the critic, as did John Wimber and others. Though the critic was reluctant to concede the wrong of the report as a whole, he later wrote a letter conceding the godliness of Paul Cain and the reality of his exceptional gifting.

JOHN WHITE

ACKNOWLEDGMENTS

I want to express my appreciation to the Kansas City Fellowship for permitting me to quote from their unedited tapes and so on. I must also put into print my very warm thanks to my wife Mary, my daughter Debby and her husband John, and the following good friends: Brian and Gill Skinner, Richard and Prue Bedwell, Peter and Ann Scott, Teddy and Margaret Saunders, and Mike Pilavachi, who have all most patiently checked my manuscript for readability and hopefully my mind for gullibility and sanity! I have been most grateful for their wise comments and kind warnings. I am also deeply indebted to David Wavre of Hodder and Stoughton for his constructive criticism and careful editing. In the end I have had to use my own judgment about the credibility of everything I am sharing within these pages. I have written as matters honestly appear to me. If the substance of what is related here is true, as I sincerely believe it is, then, however unpalatable it may be to some (as prophets and prophecy have ever tended to be), the church of Jesus Christ needs to know. Something very significant is being confronted here.

DAVID PYTCHES

INTRODUCTION TO NEW EDITION

I am delighted that Dr. John White, a greatly respected Christian teacher and writer worldwide and a dear friend from our days in Latin America, has agreed to write the foreword to this new edition.

The book has been slightly revised as a new edition for the following reasons:

First, the current attention being paid to the work developing at the Kansas City Fellowship has caused the leadership there to be particularly concerned about how they are presented. They wish to eliminate any impression of elitism for themselves. They believe only that they may become one of the many different streams of God's blessing and that the promised revival therein is for the church at large.

Second, revision has provided the opportunity for verifying my original sources for all that was written in the first edition. No major change has been necessary, but I have rectified the ages of people in a couple of instances. I have corrected details in the case of one prophecy, which was remarkably fulfilled, though the exact date was at first misreported to me. I have eliminated another, which was given and fulfilled but exaggerated with repetition over time. Its omission makes no substantial difference. Reports of supernatural experiences and personal details that were already public were included in the first edition. However, some of these have since been seen as overexposing a very sensitive area, and I have readily acceded to the request that they be taken out. Their removal in no way detracts from the retelling of the story.

One reviewer has felt that the book needed more on discernment, a subject I had already dealt with in a previous book, "Does God Speak Today?" I am now glad to repeat it in an adapted form in Appendix B, "Discerning Prophecies."

In a few places I have slightly enlarged on the historical and teaching side and otherwise rearranged material to make it more readable.

Finally, in revising this book I want to put on record the blessing I have received through my personal contact with Paul Cain and the Kansas City Fellowship (the latter now part of the Vineyard Christian Fellowship network). I have never anywhere met nor heard of such a level of proven revelation in over thirty years of traveling the world as a minister of the Gospel of Christ. In all my contacts with them, I have been profoundly impressed with their prophetic gifting; their passion for the Lord Jesus, the Cross, and the Word of God; their commitment to regular sacrificial intercession; their simple lifestyle; their generosity to the poor and to missions; their hunger and thirsting after righteousness; and their humility and grace in the face of criticism and opposition. These godly elements have been conspicuous by their absence from too many of God's people around the world today. We pray that revival, which is their vision, will restore these values once again to the church for the glory of Jesus Christ.

INTRODUCTION

A t a recent conference (August 1989) held in Denver, Colorado, which was organized for pastors worldwide of the Vineyard Christian Fellowship, Bob Jones, a prophet from Kansas City (not to be confused with the founder of a North American fundamentalist university), approached an afternoon visitor amongst the *conferencistas* and asked him what he was doing there since he was not a pastor. This was not by way of reproach but out of curiosity.

"That's correct! I am not in fact a pastor," said the intruder "and I do not pretend to be a pastor, but my son is one and I have come to visit him."

"Well," said the prophet, "it's strange, since you should not really be here, but I saw you in a vision last night. Another strange thing is that you are not a prophet either and yet you have seen the earth from the heavenlies! What is more, you have been searching for the remnants of Noah's ark on Mount Ararat but you have been looking for it in the wrong place. And you are going to find it."

Bob Jones then described the "correct" location in some detail as he had seen it in his vision, and his words seemed meaningful to the man he was addressing.

"The discovery will be a sign of a spiritual revival breaking out in that region," added the prophet.

"That's amazing!" replied the intruder. "I have in fact seen the earth from the heavenlies, since I was an astronaut and I have walked on the moon. My name is James Erwin. Furthermore, for some time now I have been leading a 'Flight Foundation Expedition' team each year to the region of Mount Ararat searching for any remains of the ark!"

Probably the reader will say that he is not impressed by this kind of report because clearly an astronaut who had walked on the moon would be easily recognizable and his pastimes well-known. This "prophet" had most likely been given the lowdown on the astronaut by the organizers of the conference or others present. There could be a number of natural explanations to account for the story. Was it really likely today that God would reveal such information directly to some "prophet"? Suffice it to say that a number of sane and reasonable people who were at the conference believed that Bob Jones actually had these facts revealed to him by God.

Bob Jones is one of a number of prophets that Christians are becoming increasingly aware of, who are apparently being raised up in the church. Whatever are we Bible-loving Christians to make of it all? Dismiss it, discuss it, or declare it?

This book combines some personal accounts of extraordinary prophecies and some personal encounters with a number of very ordinary prophets with a few biographies to set the material in context. The intention has been to show how such prophets and prophecies have already proved productive for the leadership in a local church situation. There seems to be the promise of great blessing through the availability of prophecy to the wider church.

I am attempting to show in this book how the leadership in one local church has learned to cope constructively and to great advantage with such an unaccustomed and unusual dimension and/or intrusion into its corporate life. It also reflects something of the swing of my personal reactions, from fascination and wonder to the anger of an outraged intellect; the fear of blame for possibly encouraging a plague of phony prophets or the debasing of true Christian spirituality to a "dial-a-prophecy" way of life; the threat to ecclesiastical order and the fate of ostracism from other Christian brothers: all this and then back to a gradual acceptance and a positive assessment.

The increase and impact of such "divine intelligence" through prophecy will prove a great challenge to our sophisticated church members in these days of spiritual confusion; it will also create a stimulus to holiness of life in the present climate of moral corruption once it becomes widely recognized that God is disclosing the secrets of people's hearts, even to what is being said in the director's boardroom or the king's bedroom (2 Kings 6:12). And finally it will be an evangelistic "sign . . . for unbelievers . . . he is convinced. . . . So, falling down on his face, he will worship God and report that God is truly among you" (1 Cor. 14:22–25).

Please read on!

CHAPTER ONE

KANSAS CITY AIRPORT AND A FLIGHT BACK IN HISTORY

It was Saturday, May 6, 1989. We had just flown into Kansas City following our third series of conferences arranged for us by the Episcopal Renewal Ministries at centers across the U.S. Our team included Richard and Prue Bedwell and my wife Mary and me.

It was getting late on that Saturday evening. The temperature was hot and we were weary. Mike Bickle, the leader of the Kansas City Fellowship, was arranging for someone to meet us, but as yet our suitcases had not appeared on the airline luggage conveyor belt, and we were not expecting our "collector" to materialize for a few more minutes.

I spent these waiting moments casually reflecting on how we had come to be here of all places. "This is crazy!" I thought. "What we need is a complete rest after those hectic conferences— not to start meeting a whole lot more people!" My mind flitted back to November 7, 1988, when our old friend John Wimber had come for a two-day visit to rest in our home following his recent conference in Edinburgh.

An Extraordinary Story

John had asked us if we could also host another North American pastor, a fellow speaker from that same conference.

"Hi, David," he drawled in his friendly California accent, as he introduced him. "Meet my good friend Mike Bickle. I think you'll find he has an interesting story to share."

John had never spoken a truer word! What Mike had to share with us blew my mind. He told us an extraordinary story about his experiences with some prophets. He had originally treated these prophets with very great suspicion but in the course of double-checking their revelations he had finally come round to accepting them as being from God.

Through one of them he had been led to found a new church in Kansas City six years earlier. They now had a regular attendance of about 1,500 at each of their Sunday services at the Grandview Worship Center, a building originally constructed as a sports complex. They had already branched out into five other fellowships across Kansas City (with another 1,500 membership between them) and they had a vision for planting forty-five more such fellowships in Kansas City within the next ten years.

In these days of Church decline in the West this was very exciting news indeed, and I could not resist asking if it would be possible for us to visit him and his church the next time we were in the States. Not only did he welcome the idea but he offered to provide hospitality for us. He also said he would try to arrange a meeting with some of these prophets.

The First Surprise

And now at last we were here in Kansas City and wondering what on earth we were letting ourselves in for. Suddenly there was a friendly shout and turning around we saw Mike Bickle himself coming to meet us. He was accompanied by two men who were both unknown to us. Our friend introduced the first as Geoff Grisamore, who was about twenty-seven years old. He and his newly-wed wife Mary Ellen had kindly offered their home to the four of us so that we could all be together for the weekend. Geoff was taking charge of our baggage. Then Mike introduced the other man: a medium-sized, gentle, grey-haired man aged between fifty-five and sixty.

"David," he said, "I'd like you to meet Paul Cain."

We greeted and then as Paul was shaking hands with the others Mike took me to one side. He explained that this man was one of the prophets, though he did not like being addressed as such nor did he ever refer to himself in that way.

Introductions over, we took our luggage out to the waiting car and loaded up. It seemed quite a long haul from the airport to our destination. We stopped about halfway at the place where Paul was going to stay and he got out. I had been sitting beside him in the minibus. He had seemed very relaxed and had a good sense of humor. He was tired from his travels, as we certainly were.

There being no need to make polite conversation to the now empty seat beside me, I found myself reflecting on prophets in the Christian Church down the ages. In fact I had been doing quite a lot of reading about them before leaving the U.K. It would be true to say that I was definitely intrigued but not too kindly disposed towards them. My religious upbringing had conditioned me to be suspicious. Who wants to be "conned" by a false prophet?

Prophets of the Past

History, I reflected, had not treated the prophets too well, to be sure, from the time of Montanus (*c.* 170) down to our present day. Admittedly we only know about most of them through their critics. All sorts of weird accusations had been laid to their charge, some cynically invented and others sinfully exaggerated. Having said that, however, there were undoubtedly other charges which, it would have to be admitted, were only too true. England had her fill of strange prophets. Those from the time of Oliver Cromwell (1599–1658) were especially remembered. That was supposed to be the age of the Spirit when any believer could receive a word from the Lord and speak it out!

Many free-lance prophets (some known popularly as the "Ranters") were soon up and about. Cromwell even appointed some of these as chaplains to the army. On at least half a dozen occasions between 1647 and 1654 the council meetings of the Protector himself were interrupted by prophets, apparently without protest. But while some of the prophets in circulation at the time may have been genuine, there were many others who were obviously not. Sadly but understandably it is the latter who are best remembered!

Pseudo-messiahs

In London in April 1561, John Moore was whipped and imprisoned for saying he was the Christ. Similar treatment was meted out to his companion William Jeffrey, who claimed to be St. Peter. A month later a "stranger" was set in the stocks for calling himself the "Lord of Lords and King of Kings." The following year Eliseus Hall, a draper, was arrested for assuming the title of "Eli, the Carpenter's Son" and claiming to have had a vision from God following a two-day return visit to heaven and hell.

In 1586 a shoemaker from Essex named John White claimed to be John the Baptist, while Ralph Purden, a minister from the same county, was claiming that he would lead the saints to

Jerusalem. The next year Miles Fry, alias Emmanuel Plantagenet, believed that he was the son of Queen Elizabeth by God the Father and that his authority was greater than the Angel Gabriel's. Usually such self-appointed "prophets" were dismissed as mentally ill, but the threat to law and order prompted the attention of the authorities.

William Hacket, a discharged soldier and bankrupt illiterate, persuaded himself in 1591 that he was the "Messiah" who had come to judge the world on God's behalf. He proceeded to travel around London with two disciples, Edmund Copinger and Henry Arthrington—one he appointed a "prophet" of mercy and the other a "prophet" of judgment. Between them they publicly challenged the highest authority in the land.

Yet another "Messiah" was Wightman, an Anabaptist and Arian (today's equivalent of a Jehovah's Witness), who in 1612 became the last Englishman to be burned at the stake for heresy. He claimed to be the prophet Elijah, foretold in Malachi (4:5), and warned that those who denied his claims would be mauled to death by wild bears just like those young louts who mocked Elijah's successor, Elisha (2 Kings 2:24). These threats did not save Wightman from a cruel execution.

Power to Inflict Plagues!

The antics of these "Messiahs" were closely paralleled by the case of the two weavers, Richard Farnham and John Bull, who attracted a good deal of public attention in 1636. They too claimed to be divinely inspired prophets but with this difference: they were armed with powers to inflict plagues upon mankind and the knowledge of all things to come. "I am one of the Two Witnesses spoken of in the eleventh chapter of Revelation," declared Farnham. "The Lord has given me the power for the opening and the shutting of the heavens." Notwithstanding, both men were locked up in very earthly prisons and died there in 1642. This was not before they had issued promises to their followers that they would rise again and reign forever.

The claim to be the Two Witnesses of Revelation (chapter 11) was revived later by the tailors John Reeves and Lodwick Muggleton who established a small sect during Cromwell's time, announcing themselves to be the forerunners of Christ endowed with the keys of heaven and hell.

Enter the Women

The best known of the prophetesses before the Civil War was Lady Eleanor Davis (later Douglas) the daughter of the Earl of Castledown, who was married first to Sir John Davis and then Sir Archibald Douglas. In 1625 she claimed to hear a word, a "Voice from Heaven" early in the morning, speaking as through a trumpet: "There is nineteen years and a half to the Judgement Day." From then until her death in 1652 she was continuously given to such prophetic utterances and spent many spells in prison for her pains.

She was believed to have accurately predicted the deaths of several leading public figures as well as that of her first husband. Her ecstatic and utterly enigmatic pronouncements were frequently printed and as frequently suppressed. In a commentary she wrote on Daniel in 1633 she made dark predictions about the fate of Archbishop Laud and Charles I. Her commentary was published illegally in Amsterdam, and for this she was fined and imprisoned by the High Commission.

Some years later she went berserk in Lichfield Cathedral, defiling the altar hangings and proclaiming from the bishop's throne that she was the Primate of all England! No one, of course, could be deceived but she had to be restrained. However, she was not without serious supporters including the politician Edward Dering, who fully accepted that she had genuine foreknowledge.

The refugee Queen of Bohemia and the Anglican divine Peter de Moulin were also her champions.

Shortcut to Free Speech

Prophetesses were becoming quite the thing. This may have been partly because within the culture of the times women had no other accepted medium for public expression. The same of course was true for working-class men and probably explains why so many of them also adopted the convenient but counterfeit guise of the prophet. A readily available "word from the Lord" gave the message immediate authentication and was the best guarantee that one's voice would be heard whenever and wherever one wanted.

Jane Hawkins, a Huntingdonshire woman, had visions of the downfall of the bishops of the Church of England in 1629! Grace Carey, a Bristol widow, claimed to be seeing visions as early as 1639 which forewarned of the coming Civil War. She followed the king around urging him to make reforms before it was too late! For this and further fascinating research into the Ranters and others the reader is referred to Professor Keith Thomas's *Religion and the Decline of Magic* (especially chapter 5 on Prayer and Prophecy).

The Church was hardly prepared for the novelty of such prophets. Some were for believing them; others for banning them. John Owen, a moderate and scholarly Puritan appointed by Cromwell to be vice-chancellor of Christ Church, Oxford, was the first theologian to produce a thorough biblical treatise on the person and work of the Holy Spirit. The book, *Pneumatologia*, was an attempt to introduce some godly order on the subject.

Fifth Monarchy Men

The whole prophetic phenomenon of the Ranters lasted about thirty years and only faded with the fall of the Fifth Monarchy

Men. They had supported Cromwell during the time of the Commonwealth. These fanatics believed the time had come for the fulfillment of Daniel's prophecy concerning a fifth and messianic kingdom to follow those of Babylon, Persia, Greece, and Rome. When these Fifth Monarchy Men saw their hopes fading they suddenly rose and terrorized London. For this they were quickly put down and with them prophecy also.

North America Also

Prophecy was soon to become a problem in North America following George Whitefield's first visit (1737–38). The focus of this problem was a certain James Davenport (1716–57), a graduate of Yale, who had suffered a breakdown while still a student. This did not prevent him from entering the ministry of the church, where he gained a reputation as "a most heavenly-minded man." He joined the "Awakening" movement with fervent zeal. He soon believed he was receiving direct revelations from God, and there is no real reason to doubt that he was favored with dreams and visions. His preaching was frequently followed by "convulsions and faintings" (which today we would probably see as simply being overwhelmed by the Holy Spirit). Davenport had a chronic health problem, but this did not deter him from increased spiritual disciplines. He would spend whole nights in prayer and on one occasion preached for twenty-one hours. He influenced a number of others who, like him, claimed to be receiving direct revelations from God. Divisions occurred in homes, churches, and communities following their preaching. The effect has been seen as a threat to hijack the spiritual "Awakening."

Whitefield was blamed (in absentia) for both the extremism and the divisions, since he himself had spoken on "impressions" and thus he was suspected to have claimed direct revelations for himself also (which may or may not have been the case). Even so, Whitefield was critical and wrote, "many good souls, both clergy and laity . . . mistaking fancy for faith and imagination for revelation, were guilty of great imprudence." Whitefield was able to clarify his own position concerning Davenport and his followers on his return visit (1740–41), and confidence in this gifted young English preacher was restored. (See Arnold A. Dallimore, *George Whitefield;* London, 1990, pp. 153–155.)

The American religious leadership discovered an unexpected side effect from the large open-air revival meetings—that of the power of the masses. On the occasion of Davenport's arrest for urging his followers to defy the law, the "magistrates" required protection from the militia for fear of the mass of his "enthusiastic" supporters. Similar fears were reflected in the repressive laws passed in England following the Ranter uprising nearly a century earlier (op.cit.).

Prophecy and Social Change

Prophecy had become associated with social revolution. Religious freedom was perceived as having gone too far! The restoration of the monarchy saw the introduction of much restrictive legislation: the Corporation Act, the Quaker Act, the Act of Uniformity, and the Five Mile Act. The governing classes were determined to prevent the possibility of any return to the situation that had prevailed during the years of Cromwell's Commonwealth.

But in spite of all the abuses of prophecy through the ages there must have been some good reason why a man of the distinction of Tertullian had thrown in his lot with Montanus; or why the Wittenberg professor Andreas Carlstadt, a colaborer in the Reformation with Martin Luther, had supported Claus Storch and Thomas Munzer, prophets of the oppressed peasants in Zwichau.

9

Montanus, "the mouthpiece of the paraclete," was appealing for purity in a church which was degenerating through sophistication and formalism. Munzer was appealing to the Reformation leaders for their open support and protest against the oppression of the peasants, which was prevailing so ruthlessly at that time (1520). Both, it would seem, were raising issues which needed redress.

Evidence of Genuine Revelationary Gifting

History does not lack good plain examples of wholesome prophetic utterance. In his booklet on Divine Guidance (published privately in 1947) the late G. H. Lang cites the case of John Welsh, a covenanting minister of Ayr, who was asked by the city officials during the time of the plague of 1665 to advise whether two merchants should be admitted to trade. Removing his hat and looking upwards, he prayed quietly and then advised that they be not admitted, asserting that the plague was in their packs. The merchants then went on to another town some sixteen miles away and sold their goods; forthwith such an infection developed that the living were hardly able to bury the dead.

"Of this man of God," says Lang, "there are narrated in 'The Scots Worthies' (which to date I have been unable to trace) various other instances of similar prophetic insight and announcements." Lang cites the case also of a particular nobleman, who promised to put a certain petition before King James in London but forgot to do so. He informed Welsh that he had presented it but had received no answer. Welsh replied, "Nay, my Lord, you should not lie to God, and to me, for I know you never delivered it, though I warned you to take heed not to undertake it except you would perform it; but because you have dealt so unfaithfully, remember that God will take from you both estate and honors, and give them to your neighbour in your own time. . . ." This accordingly came to pass, for both his estate and honors were in his own time transferred to James Stuart, a cadet, but not the lineal heir of the family!

Enthusiasts

Through the centuries there were many illuminist and millenarian movements inspired by prophetic leaders, each flourishing briefly under the general description of "Enthusiasts." These nearly always reflected a yearning for a purer church and a closer relationship with God. A Jesuit historian has discerned a close similarity between all these movements: "The hypothesis of a genuine connection is almost irresistible" (Ronald A. Knox, *Enthusiasm*). Could there be something of the Holy Spirit behind this "connection," we ask?

In his book *The Ante-Nicene Fathers* (1895) F. J. A. Hort selected five main characteristics of such movements, which I have slightly edited. Their similarity with what is happening today is significant. The characteristics are:

1. A strong faith in the Holy Spirit as the promised paraclete present as a heavenly power in the church of the day.
2. A belief that the Holy Spirit was manifesting himself supernaturally through entranced prophets and prophetesses.
3. An inculcation of an especially stern and exacting standard of Christian morality and discipline in the teachings of these prophets.
4. A tendency to set up prophets against bishops. (The Montanists saw real spiritual danger in the apparently accommodating role of the episcopate to the powers of the state.)
5. An eager anticipation of the Lord's second coming as imminent and a consequent indifference to ordinary human affairs.

Contemporary Wave of Prophecy

The recent Latter Rain Movement in the United States exemplifies all the characteristics outlined by Hort above. Following a spiritual outpouring in North America during the late forties and early fifties, a surge of prophetic ministry accompanied this movement. Many were astounded by the depth of revelation about people and situations and thousands were blessed by the prophetic words to themselves and their families.

Serious problems soon arose, however, when prophecy became the "in" thing and people began to manufacture their own "prophetic" words out of their own conjectures (Ezek. 13:2). Pure revelation usually emanates from an intimate relationship with God (Jer. 23:22 and Matt. 5:8). Proper checks and balances to discern the difference between the former and the latter were never built into the development of this ministry. It seems that such a subjective area is always liable to great abuse. Jeremiah's criticism from earlier times was still applicable:

The prophets prophesy falsely . . . and My people love to have it so (Jer. 5:31).

They make you worthless; they speak a vision of their own heart, not from the mouth of the LORD (Jer. 23:16).

I have not sent these prophets, yet they ran. I have not spoken to them, yet they prophesied (Jer. 23:21).

Indeed they are prophets of the deceit of their own heart (Jer. 23:26).

[They] use their tongues and say "He says" (Jer. 23:31).

[They] prophesy false dreams . . . and cause My people to err by their lies and by their recklessness. Yet I did not send them or command them (Jer. 23:32).

This must be a recurring problem wherever prophecy is encouraged. Little was done apparently to correct such abuses effectively in the prophetic wave of the fifties in the North American churches.

The Latter Rain Movement, whatever its merits, was greatly undermined by such unbridled prophetic utterances. Men and women were prophesying all kinds of words over people but were not operating under authority. Their prophecies went untested. God is not the author of such confusion. There is a divine order for these things (1 Cor. 14:31). We all need to learn how to behave ourselves in the household of God (1 Tim. 3:15). Because these principles were overlooked, the whole movement was eventually banned from the Assemblies of God. Outsiders were left reflecting ruefully, "If the Pentecostalists can't handle this, who can?" And God's true gift of prophecy, which could have been recovered and prophets retained by the Church for blessing, was rejected along with it.

Lack of Policy for Developing Prophecy

The church has yet to develop a constructive policy for regulating prophetic activity within her ranks—a need first frankly recognized in the *Didache* (written sometime between the first and the third century), which dealt with the problem too crudely to be helpful. A policy was still needed for dealing with prophecy without quenching the Spirit (1 Thess. 5:19) to encourage its development appropriately. However, no generally acceptable way had yet been advocated, probably because prophets have never been generally acceptable! (2 Chron. 18:7*b*; Hos. 9:7*b*). Their messages (even when genuine) have too often proved disagreeable (Jer. 15:10), especially to people who have itching ears only for what they themselves want to hear (2 Tim. 4:3), rather than what the Spirit is saying to the churches (Rev. 3:22).

Rule-of-thumb Approach

The simple and spontaneous rule-of-thumb reaction through the centuries seems to have been to vilify and persecute the prophets themselves—an age-old practice which the Lord himself thoroughly condemned. This nihilist approach has dominated the perceptions of the Church throughout history. How often have we been reminded of the good Bishop Butler's famous words to John Wesley after their meeting in 1739 when he said: "Pretending to extraordinary revelations from the Holy Ghost is a horrid thing, a very horrid thing!"

There are no records available of direct contributions from the Montanists and Anabaptists themselves to help the modern-day researcher. We do not even know if Montanus or the later Anabaptists ever committed their own prophecies or views to paper (though we know there are some prophecies attributed to individuals among them). Therefore mainly negative impressions remain on subliminal recall to snuff out spontaneously any hint of ongoing supernatural revelation for the church of today.

"The chief effect of Montanism on the Catholic church was greatly to reinforce the conviction that revelation had come to an end with the apostolic age, and so to foster the creation of a closed canon of the New Testament," wrote Henry Chadwick (*The Early Church,* p. 15). Thereafter most believers assumed that the completion of the New Testament was the limit of God's revelation and to all practical purposes taught that God would never speak again except through the Bible. The idea of a modern-day prophet who believed he had received revelations directly from God for himself, another individual, or the church would be a matter of ridicule in most ecclesiastical quarters today.

Somewhat surprisingly, a most readable and relevant discussion concerning the dilemma over prophecy comes from a secular source. In the first half of this century the playwright George Bernard Shaw took it upon himself to represent the fascinating story of the fifteenth century French maiden Joan of Arc. Both his preface and the play *Saint Joan* are well worth reading to clarify thinking on the far-reaching implications for the church regarding revelations believed to be direct from God. The nineteen-year-old Joan was burned as a heretic in 1431 and canonized a saint nearly five hundred years later in 1920.

Was the Age of Revelation Over?

Professor Chadwick names Irenaeus as "the last writer who can still think of himself as belonging to the eschatological age of miracle and revelation." Born about A.D. 125, Irenaeus was Bishop of Lyons from A.D. 177 to 202. It is instructive to read what Irenaeus himself wrote, since his life and ministry are supposed to have rounded off a defined period of church history. We may find his actual words on the subject in his work *Against Heresies,* where he says:

> For which cause also His true disciples, having received grace from Him, use it in His name for the benefit of the rest of mankind, even as each has received the gifts from Him. For some certainly do drive out demons so that those who have been cleansed from evil spirits frequently both believe and join themselves to the church. (Book I)
>
> Others have *foreknowledge of things to be, and visions and prophetic speech* [italics mine], and others cure the sick by the laying on of hands and make them whole. Yea, moreover, as I have said, the dead even have been raised up and remained among us for many years. And what shall I say more? It is not possible to name the number of gifts which the church throughout the world has received from God in the name of Jesus Christ. (Book V; Eusebius, *Ecclesiastical History,* chap. vii, A.D. 316.)

It was not that Irenaeus had any problems about accepting a canon of Scripture then in the process of being recognized; indeed, he was one of the first defenders of the concept. He recognized the real value of a "canon" or fixed list of authoritative writings of approved orthodoxy, especially in his fight against heresy. But it is plain that Irenaeus, like both Tertullian and Montanus, was convinced that the living God was still speaking to the church through revelations of the Holy Spirit according to His promises contained within the New Testament canon.

Early Church Prophets

Jesus promised to send prophets (Matt. 23:34) and warned against false prophets (Matt. 7:15 and Matt. 24:24). He encouraged the church to be receptive to prophets (Matt. 10:41). Active prophets are mentioned by name in the New Testament: Agabus in Acts 11:28, Judas and Silas in Acts 15:32, and a number of others in Acts 13:1.

After his ascension the victorious Christ endowed the church and "gave . . . some to be prophets"—an office which was distinct from that of the evangelist, pastor, teacher, or apostle, who were all to prepare God's people for works of service so that the Body of Christ might be built up (Eph. 4:11–12). He also sent his Holy Spirit at Pentecost and through the Spirit the nine "spiritual gifts" (spelled out in 1 Cor. 12:7–11) were manifested in the New Testament church. One of these (which is to be eagerly desired [1 Cor. 14:1–3]), was the gift of prophecy (1 Cor. 12:10). Later in the same chapter Paul explains how (in the Church) God has appointed prophets (1 Cor. 12:28), among others. Then through his questions (1 Cor. 12:29, 30), Paul shows clearly that not all are prophets—but by the same token prophets would have been there somewhere!

Prophets are identified in the fall of Babylon, reflecting the approaching end of the age. Babylon's ruin will be the cause for rejoicing by the prophets, who will presumably be living witnesses of that event (Rev. 18:20). The blood of prophets within her (presumably latter-day ones) will also testify to her wickedness (Rev. 18:24).

16

Paul had prophecies made over him by Ananias (Acts 2:14), by other prophets (Acts 13:1), and by Agabas (Acts 21:10, 11). Timothy clearly had something similar (1 Tim. 1:18; 4:14). Paul urges the church not to treat prophecies with contempt. Prophets were clearly never infallible, which is why Paul says, "Test all things; hold fast what is good" (1 Thess. 5:21). Neither were prophets omniscient: "We prophesy in part" (1 Cor. 13:9), says Paul. But, nevertheless, he encourages Christians to seek the gift with eagerness (1 Cor. 14:1, 39).

Some Definitions

Prophecy, understood in its broadest sense, may be seen in six ways:

1. Simply addressing a person or speaking about a situation with a clearly inspired word.
2. Preaching under the anointing of God.
3. Unfolding facts about the future from the Scriptures, i.e., teaching on the second coming of Christ, the last days, and the final judgment.
4. Addressing social issues. Clearly there are people raised up by God who have a gift for discerning evils directly causing oppression, etc.
5. Discerning the signs of the times in the light of Scripture.
6. Communicating revelations from God through dreams, visions, angelic visitations, audible voices, etc. It is mainly to this latter area that we address ourselves in this book.

A Present-day Prophet

Paul Cain would certainly fall into the category of a present-day prophet. Unlike the others that Mike Bickle had mentioned with gifts for prophesying, Paul did not live in Kansas City but came from Dallas. It was there that he had received revelations from the Lord which had been forwarded by telephone to John Wimber in Los Angeles (though the two had never actually met) via a third party. This was during the time of a leadership crisis in the Vineyard Christian Fellowship at Anaheim, which John Wimber had founded ten years earlier. He had been astounded at the insight of Paul Cain who had provided him with such very perceptive information, which Paul could not possibly have gained from any human source. In spite of his doubts about the availability of such a high level of revelation from God to the church today, the precision of this message persuaded John to take Paul's very wise advice seriously—and wise indeed it proved to be, as events at Anaheim turned out.

Realizing that this must be the very man John Wimber had described to us back in the U.K., we felt pleased now that we had been able to meet Paul Cain, and even more delighted to learn that he was booked by Mike Bickle to preach on the following evening at the Kansas City Fellowship worship center where we had planned to be. It was going to be an interesting weekend.

LITTLE BROTHER
—THE BOY PROPHET

W e were very much looking forward to hearing Paul Cain preach on the Sunday evening and arrived to find the church already packed. It was clear that his ministry was well known and highly respected in Kansas City. Before Paul preached a lady gave a remarkable testimony.

She described a visit she had received from Paul Cain, whom she had never met before, while she was a long-term patient in a mental institution in California some years earlier. Her story of miraculous restoration to health followed by her discharge within a matter of days served admirably to raise the level of faith of the congregation. Paul was then given the microphone to address us.

Our Disappointment

It is difficult for me to say what I thought. I had to admit I was disappointed. His style was reminiscent of some of the Pentecostal preachers I had heard during my time of missionary service in Chile, but I was cross with myself for feeling antagonistic over his presentation. There were amazing swings in his style that certainly made one listen attentively.

Flights of sheer oratory and profound scriptural insight poured forth, followed by solemn calls to repentance, righteousness, and holiness of life. One felt that heaven was about to descend and both the glory and the judgment of God would burst upon us at any moment.

On the other hand he was certainly no expository or orderly preacher. Intermittently he would crack some corny quip, alternating with frequent apologies for being confused, then groaning over an apparent physical affliction that was troubling him—the kind of drawing attention to oneself that makes the average Briton cringe slightly. We had heard that he suffered from a weak heart and feared a collapse was imminent.

Was it Our Fault?

Now that I think I understand these things a little better I suspect the confusion and pain that was inflicted upon him originated from our direction. We had been introduced to him as good friends but were feeling pretty uptight with our many criticisms and disappointments. Some of the negative energy from this was probably disturbing his sensitive soul. We had no idea at that stage that he could perceive our thoughts.

We learned later that at another conference, where there were over 3,000 in attendance, he had become aware of the presence of three hostile people somewhere in the crowd. They were spies from a certain seminary in another state and had come in looking for data to destroy his reputation. He knew their names by revelation from God. He knew where they had come from and what their criticisms were without ever having met them. He mentioned that he was aware of their presence and motives in the course of his address but did not publicly identify them and the men in question did not reveal themselves.

Someone else present told him afterwards that he had recognized the people concerned who were personally known to him. When Paul Cain then named them, the friend corrected him over the first name of one of them; but it turned out that Paul was right—it was simply that the man was not commonly known by his first name, which was the one that had been revealed to Paul.

Affront to Rationality

Our overall problem seemed to be the sheer effrontery of Paul's approach to our rational minds. In the end he closed apologetically, seeming suddenly to give up. There had been no clearly anointed ministry to conclude, as had obviously been anticipated by many of the congregation including ourselves. We went home to ponder it all. "Whatever was all that about?" we wondered!

We were beginning to hear the strangest of stories concerning Paul Cain. My curiosity was getting the better of me and I was determined to find out why this gentle and humble man with the silver hair and the sometimes golden tongue was held in such high esteem by these people.

Mike Bickle had warned us to beware if we wanted to get to the real truth. When it came to encounters with God, Paul was a master of the understatement and tended to downplay everything. Paul does not want to be referred to as a prophet—he does not like anything that might tempt him to think more highly than any Christian ought to think of himself. He especially abhors anything that hints of superstardom in the Church. His master and model is Jesus Christ who made himself of no reputation.

This is one of the dangers of writing a book like this: people might try to put Paul Cain on a pedestal. That would be counterproductive to the message Paul is bringing to the Church: that the day of the superstars is over; that God will not share the glory that belongs to him; and that he is looking for humility. He sees that God is deliberately operating today through a new breed of workers—ordinary, dedicated laypeople. Paul wants everyone to know that he too is simply an ordinary, earthen vessel and nothing more. Mike Bickle, who knows Paul well, says that when Paul indicates that the Lord wants him to say or do something this may come out of an angelic visitation.

A Miracle Baby

His fascinating story began in 1929, one of the most turbulent years in recent U.S. history, when Paul was still in the womb of Anna Cain, his forty-five-year-old mother. His Jewish father, William Henry Cain, fifty-six and poor, eked out a living as a steamboat operator on the Mississippi River and later a worker on the railway. His mother was sick with heart problems, besides being "terminally" ill with tuberculosis. She also had cancerous tumors in her uterus and breasts. She was taken from her home in Garland, a small farming community about twenty miles from Dallas, Texas, to Baylor University Hospital at Dallas. The doctors, however, pronounced her incurable and she was discharged. She returned to Garland to die.

Once home among the cotton fields and the birch trees she took her cause to Jesus. She had a strong faith in the Lord. Like Hannah (in 1 Sam. 1:11), she promised to dedicate her offspring to the Lord. She cried out to him until, at the hour past midnight (ever a sacred hour to her from that day to this), the Lord appeared in the form of an angel. Touching her on the shoulder with his right hand he made her a wonderful promise: "Daughter, be of good cheer, you shall live and not die. The fruit of your womb is a male child whom I shall anoint to preach my gospel like the Apostle Paul; and you shall name him Paul."

Her healing was immediate. Specialists reported it as the first time they had seen new tissue restored to diseased breasts. When the time came she gave birth to a baby boy, just as the Lord had said, and of course she called him Paul. He was nursed at the very breasts which had so recently been riddled with cancer. Her doctor called her a miracle woman. She is now, at the time of writing, in her one hundred and fifth year!

God Called Him by Name

Anna Cain never talked to Paul about the Lord's call upon his life until the Lord himself had revealed this directly to him when he was eight years old. As a child Paul was misunderstood by other children because he did not enjoy the same things as they did. He was nicknamed "Droopy Eyes" and was terribly shy. Even then he was aware of a supernatural power which guided many of his actions and as early as he could remember he wanted to be a preacher. Paul had already had a conversion experience at the age of eight, which gave him, to use his own words, an insatiable love for Jesus. He soon found himself taking long walks through the cotton fields with Jesus.

One evening as he was worshipping in his local Baptist church he became especially conscious of the Lord's presence upon him. This feeling stayed with him all the way home, and when he reached the house he had a sense that somehow God was going to speak to him. Suddenly he heard the Lord call his name! In utter terror he rushed for cover under the bedclothes.

Thinking she might be protecting him his fourteen-year-old sister Mildred asked the Lord to speak to her instead! But the Lord had an audible message for the boy under the bedclothes. His sister heard it all and has ever since been a committed lifetime supporter of Paul's ministry. Paul Cain has never shared with anyone all the sacred burden of that message except to say that if he kept himself pure the Lord promised him a ministry which would reach the masses—that he would preach the gospel through healing.

Having heard his mother recount the miracle of her own healing, without which he could never have been born, combined with his personal commission from the Lord to heal, it is not surprising that Paul Cain has never had a problem in believing in divine healing. Paul's mother, grandmother, and great-grandmother had all been born with the gift of "seeing." His great-grandmother would sometimes see things in broad daylight and ask her friends or family if they could see them too. If they said they could not, she would occasionally lay her hand upon them and they would immediately see the identical vision. This seems very similar, in effect, to Elisha's prayer for his servant (2 Kings 6:17) when he prayed that the Lord would open the servant's eyes to see what Elisha saw—and he did.

Paul now found he was "seeing" also and would know things that were going to happen to classmates at school or were happening to absent friends. He knew simple things like who would end up with a bloody nose or who would win a race, and the other children recognized that what Paul said came true. Paul, the eight-year-old, had also become an avid reader of the New Testament. His class teacher was very understanding, when he was in the fourth grade she appointed him "chaplain" and he would read the Bible and preach to his class! He was of course regarded as abnormal among his peers. He found this difficult to come to terms with for a long time. He resented being different and found himself beginning to withdraw from people. He jokes about it now: "For years I resented being abnormal but when I found out what being normal was I wanted to be abnormal again!"

Preaching to Spikes

Knowing he was going to be an evangelist Paul used to go out into the backyard to preach. He would collect discarded railway spikes, the large-headed kind used for pinning rails to wooden sleepers. He would arrange these spikes in rows like people sitting in pews. His childhood dream of a big congregation was easily satisfied. He would simply go out and collect more spikes to increase the attendance at his meetings. Then he would preach to them over and over again. He said there was never any response—they were too hard-headed—but at least they could not get away!

Paul claims to have built his first "church" by the time he was nine years old! He used fencing boards for the walls and his aunt gave him some whitewash to paint them. But the place badly needed a roof. There was an outhouse in their backyard which Paul did not think was being put to much good use at the time and which had a roof. It was a nicely shingled roof just like any proper church would have. Paul, with the help of some of his classmates, moved it from the outhouse to cover his church. Before his new church could ever be dedicated, however, he was to receive the biggest whipping of his life from his father. Mr. Cain insisted that the roof was needed right where it had come from!

By this time his Baptist pastor had also discovered that Paul was seeing and hearing things which others apparently could not see and hear. He could see when a person was going to be healed and live and also knew when someone was going to die. This made him feel very uncomfortable. Despite Paul's tender years, the Rev. Dr. Parish began to take him out with him on his pastoral visits. Paul would know—perhaps by how people were dressed in his visions—which ones the Lord was going to heal when they prayed for them. One incident Paul recalls from those early days was the case of Mary. Long before they reached the hospital he described to his pastor that in one ward they would meet a lady of about sixty robed in a rose-colored housecoat. She would be in bed dying with cancer and at the foot of the bed would be her brother Tom, standing dressed in his working clothes. When they arrived at the ward they saw the scene exactly as Paul had described it and when they prayed for Mary she was healed, just as Paul had predicted. Dr. Parish encouraged Paul to keep his eyes on God's call to be a preacher, though this was hardly necessary under the circumstances.

Paul's Public Ministry

By the age of nine "Little Brother" (as he was being affectionately referred to by adults, perhaps because it was the form of address used by the angel who spoke to him from time to time) began public preaching in a limited way. He had gathered a "big" crowd of about ten or twelve neighborhood kids along with his grandmother and his parents, and they sang and praised God at his meetings. Public preaching for a boy of that age was something, not surprisingly, which the Baptists found hard to handle. Increasingly Paul was being invited to evangelistic healing meetings run by Pentecostals. Their leaders seemed to have fewer problems about a boy prophet, as they called him, having seen the anointing of the Lord upon him.

About five hundred people attended Paul's first big preaching meeting in Dallas. When he stood up in front he became so frightened that he started shaking and could not speak! The people believed that such fearful shaking was a sign of the Holy Spirit's presence upon him (though Paul Cain imagined it was sheer fright), and they began to rush forward confessing their sins and getting saved and healed. The young Paul stood watching in amazed silence as he continued shaking for about thirty minutes before he sat down. The next day the news spread that revival was breaking out at the young preacher's meetings!

By the time Paul was about eighteen he had a regular radio ministry and was conducting healing services in a small tent.

He began traveling across America ministering as an evangelist and healer. Those were the early days of the healing movement which swept through the Pentecostal churches during the forties and fifties under the leadership of evangelists like William Branham, Oral Roberts, T. L. Osborn, A. A. Allen, Jack Coe, and many others well known in those days.

Though he could not really understand why, Paul began to find himself resented and even rejected by some of the leaders (not necessarily any of those named above). Possibly this was because they felt his youthfulness tended to bring discredit on the healing movement; possibly it was because he still had much to learn of the Christian graces and had not yet matured into that model of spiritual discretion and sensitive diplomacy which is so much the mark of the Paul Cain one meets today. But then again, possibly, though Paul does not say so, the resentment was present because of the extraordinary anointing that was upon him, and jealousy was a factor.

William Branham's Story

However, one man who encouraged him greatly was the late William Branham, now regarded as the pioneer of the postwar healing revival. There were strong similarities in their "anointings," an often-used word which calls for an explanation. In my own particular Christian tradition we hardly ever use the word in the sense intended here. This kind of "anointing" is the clear manifestation of the working of the Holy Spirit in a person through revelations, prophecy, and supernatural signs.

Such an anointing was certainly upon William Branham. He was born in 1909. His parents were poor and his home was a dirt-floor log cabin built in the Kentucky hills. Although he was apparently the child of non-Christian parents an extraordinary light appeared in the room where he lay newborn. This did not last long, but long enough to be the talk of his neighborhood for many years to come.

Then, when he was three, he received a divine visitation that was followed by another when he was seven. He was making his way back from the well to his home when he was attracted by loud rustling in a leafy poplar tree beside the path. He looked up and saw what appeared to be the effect of a mighty wind in the tree but then noticed that other trees nearby were not touched by it. Curious, the little boy stood still, peering at it more intently. Suddenly he heard the awesome roar of a voice and recognized his own name. The young William was terrified and rushed home as fast as his legs would carry him. Once there he hid himself under the bedclothes, never moving till the following morning.

Some years later, after experiencing a personal healing, Branham received the call to preach through an angel and became an independent Baptist pastor. His ministry was blessed by a revival in Jeffersonville, Indiana, where he later built a large tabernacle.

Branham did not actually hear that voice again for thirty years. Then one day he happened to be in a cave and the voice sounded forth once more, the same voice he had heard when he was seven. As a result of this visitation in 1946 Branham was given power to discern people's illnesses and the secrets of their hearts.

Legend of Spiritual Power

In his *All Things are Possible: the healing and charismatic revivals in modern America* (1975), D. E. Harrell, Jr., says that "The power of a Branham service . . . remains a legend unparalleled in the history of the charismatic movement." This assessment is further attested in *The Pentecostals* (1977) by Walter J. Hollenweger, who once acted as Branham's interpreter in

Zurich. Hollenweger wrote that he was "not aware of any case in which he (Branham) was mistaken in the often detailed statements that he made." These details concerned the people who were about to be healed.

When Branham conducted his packed healing meetings, orderly queues would form beside him and he would preach in between ministering to the sick. Sometimes he would seem to be searching for something to say; if one was unaware of his way of ministering it was helpful to hear him remind the people that he could not pray for their healing until the angel of the Lord had appeared to him. He would say to the public, "You all know what I am waiting for. I can't do anything until he comes." Once he had the assurance of the angel's presence Branham would turn to the person and tell him details concerning himself and also the nature of his complaint, all of which apparently was being revealed to him supernaturally. He would then lay hands on the person quickly and tell him to go his way—he was healed! Invariably this would prove to be the case.

Branham died in 1965, having taken his prophetic preaching and ministry of healing and deliverance to the far corners of the earth right to the end of his life.

Recently my wife and I were fortunate enough to see some early TV recordings of Branham and his public ministry, and were pleasantly surprised by the self-effacing character of this humble but extraordinary man of God—so very much in contrast to many (though certainly not all) of the latter-day, image-minded TV evangelists in the U.S. By all accounts William Branham lived moderately and dressed modestly. There was no suggestion of showmanship in those films that we saw.

A Special Bond

There was a special bond between William Branham and Little Brother in the early days of Paul's ministry. Branham would often engage Paul's help. The older man would open a healing mission in a certain city and then leave after a few days. There would be a twenty-four-hour overlap when both were together and then Paul would take over for the last few days. Sometimes, when Branham could not meet a commitment, he would send Paul in his place.

The extent of their spiritual "sight" was phenomenal. When they called each other by phone one would often say to the other in fun, "You're all right today. How am I?" and each would know the other's state of health precisely.

On one occasion after Mike Bickle had been complaining to his wife that he had "a bit of a sniffle" or a slight cold—something he rarely had—the phone rang. Bickle picked up the receiver and heard Paul on the line. He had heard about Paul's gift so he said by way of a joke, "Hi, Paul! You're all right today! How am I?" Immediately Paul answered him, "Why, Mike, you've got a bit of a sniffle and you are all wet. Your hair is standing up on the left side of your head."

Bickle called his wife Diane to look at him. "Sweetheart, Paul says I have a 'sniffle,' I am all wet, and my hair is standing up on one side. Am I all wet?"

"Yes," she said. "You've just come out of the shower!"

"And is my hair standing up on one side?"

"Yes," she replied, "on the left side!"

I included this story in the first edition as one of what Paul quaintly calls "little tokens" from the Lord that he has often been given to show that the "line is still open." Paul has since told me that in this case it was a gentle warning from the Lord to Mike that he should take care of his health.

Some Unorthodox Teachings

It is important for the record to say that though Dr. Hollenweger was not aware of any case where Branham "was mistaken in the often detailed statements that he made," he was undoubtedly referring to the revelations which Branham received about situations, circumstances, and people he was ministering to, and not to all his doctrinal statements. Here it seems that in his later years Branham may have fallen into serious error.

Due partly to ignorance (arising from his lack of any theological training), and isolation (arising out of his style of revelatory leadership), corrective theological insights were not easily available to him. Neither could he have been immune to the inevitable temptations concerning his own "superior" knowledge and ministry, which may have blinded his judgment in some areas.

Whether he was actually at fault or not, history is clear that Branham's unique record became tarnished with some unbiblical teachings. These have been attributed to him by some responsible leaders—though his supporters claim they were the work of others who exploited his good name (such as some of his followers formed a sect called the Branhamites after his death). These have been further distorted by later detractors. In any case no man is infallible, however effective or remarkable.

Paul Cain claims personally to have been unaware of false teaching in Branham but that could have been because he rarely ministered with Branham laterally, but only in his place. Whatever the case may be, Paul has openly and completely dissociated himself from any of the strange or unorthodox teaching attributed to Branham either during or after his lifetime. He does remember Branham being seriously worried over some of his "followers" who referred to him as "Elijah." He had mentioned this to Paul in person and remarked that if they persisted in that sort of thing the Lord would remove him. He died a few years after that very comment in a road accident.

None of this can alter the impact of an amazing healing ministry to the glory of God; nor will it alter the evangelistic impact of his simple and direct words about Jesus and the cross, which led thousands to a saving knowledge of Jesus Christ.

DISILLUSIONMENT WITH SUPERSTARDOM

When still a teenager Cain went to Tulsa, Oklahoma, certain he was led by God, to call on the Rev. Dr. Ward. The latter (later to become a firm friend and fellow speaker at conferences with Paul) was the pastor of the famous Bethel Temple (Assemblies of God), which at the time was suffering a serious decline in the size of its congregation. Paul Cain brought some personal "revelations" concerning the pastor and an offer to conduct a healing campaign to help him build up the church in Tulsa.

Obviously stunned by the accuracy of the revelations which had clearly come from the Lord, Dr. Ward replied, "Little Brother, I believe God has sent you and I will discuss it with our elders at their board meeting tonight." The next day when Paul returned to learn of their decision he heard that the answer was no. The elders clearly did not want a "little child" to lead them.

The Working of the Gift

So Paul went to another Tulsa pastor, who at one time had had a remarkable healing ministry but was now in the same town pastoring the independent Revival Tabernacle (with a much larger seating capacity than Bethel Temple) where there was another congregation also declining in numbers. Cain explained what had happened at Bethel Temple and offered his services to that pastor, who was more than convinced by yet more revelations about himself which Paul proceeded to share with him from the Lord. He arranged for Paul to begin the next Sunday.

It was during this campaign that Paul, for the first time, experienced in public the working of the "gift," as he called it. He was looking at a man in the meeting and found himself saying, "Sir! I perceive you have the faith to be healed"—and so he was. He then caught sight of a woman in a polka-dot dress and gasped out in surprise, "Oh, sister! You in the polka-dot dress—you come from San Antonio!" "Yes," she answered. (Paul was silently amazed to have been shown this accurate fragment of information.) He looked at her again and saw an amber light upon her. He called out, "Oh, Sister! Get up out of that chair!" At this she shot up, kicking over a couple of crutches in the process, and began to run round the aisles completely healed and praising God.

A mighty movement of God was soon being launched which was to reach several thousand people. Dr. Ward of Bethel Temple attended those meetings, both praising God each time he witnessed the working of God's miraculous power and wringing his hands with sadness each time he recollected that God had originally intended to bless Bethel Temple in that way and it had been his own elders who had closed the door to it.

Reading the Instructions

Nowadays Paul teaches very carefully that it is essential to "read the instructions" which come with the gift and not to get carried away as he had in those early days. He tells some embarrassing stories against himself to make the point. Very soon Paul was calling people out in public and telling them the secrets of their hearts. Not surprisingly things began to get rough for him at that stage. The pastor took him aside and said, "Little Brother, your gifting is wonderful. You are called to heal the sick but you've been pointing out the sins of some of my best members!" Paul did not realize it then, but his days in Tulsa were definitely numbered.

He had yet to understand about "the instructions"—the kind of thing that Jesus was talking about when he said to his disciples, "I still have many things to say to you, but you cannot bear them now" (John 16:12). Earlier Jesus had said to them, "The Father who sent Me gave Me a command, what I should say and what I should speak" (John 12:49). Words of knowledge sometimes need to be used with words of wisdom.

Move to Sacramento

The pastor quietly arranged for Paul to transfer to Sacramento and continue his healing ministry in California where he said the need was greater! The good pastor omitted any mention of the revelation of secrets when he commended Paul to his pastor friend in Sacramento. The first meeting there was to be held in the Governor's Hall.

Once again incredible things began to happen, as Paul Cain recalls: "I almost ruined my meeting. I jumped to my feet and pointed out one of the ushers—a real bruiser standing in the aisle. 'You old hypocrite,' the Lord says. 'How can you stand there and have anything to do with what's going on at this meeting when you know what's going on in your own heart. You are planning to go off with that lady over there [he was pointing directly at her] at the end of this week and to leave your wife over there [and he pointed now at the wife—both the wife and the other woman were totally unknown to Paul but he identified

34

them through the Spirit]. She has your three children and you are deserting them. You old hypocrite!' " The accused man began striding down the aisle towards Paul while the other ushers tried to dissuade him. "Leave him alone; he can't touch the man of God!" said Paul, who shudders now to recall how very grandly and smugly he pronounced those words. The next thing was that the usher had dropped his collecting bag and was running towards the platform. He was within a yard of Paul when he was suddenly struck down to the floor. Looking up sobbing, he cried out, "It's all true—what must I do?"

Paul then caught sight of another woman and pointing at her he said, "And you, lady, if you don't repent I'm going to tell everyone what you've been doing in room number 202 in your motel today." The woman in question fell to the floor crying out in repentance. And there was a lot more of the same to follow. Paul continued "naming people—and who was messing with whom." The power of God descended that night. When it came to the end the pastor of the church was nowhere to be seen. Paul had to dismiss the meeting himself.

The Pastor's Early Phone Call

The next morning he had an early phone call. It was a simple message relayed to him in his hotel saying that the pastor wanted him to listen to his radio broadcast just coming on the air. Paul Cain tuned in. "Folks!" said the pastor. "We are in the midst of a great revival. Last night something happened that I have never seen before. The preacher called the people out. He told them their sins, who they were committing them with, and where they were committing them. Someone said to me afterwards, 'Where were you, Pastor?' 'Well,' I admitted, 'I was under the grand piano confessing all my sins!' " So now the news was all over town.

When the pastor met Paul later he said, "Young man, we

35

must protect ourselves. If this keeps going someone's going to drop down dead like Ananias and Sapphira'' (see Acts 5:1–11). Perceiving biblical precedent the young and ever innocent Paul replied, ''Oh, that would be wonderful. Let's pray it will happen!'' ''Are you crazy?'' replied the pastor. ''They'd put us in prison.'' His heart leaping once again at the glorious prospect of sharing the fate of the early disciples, Paul responded, ''Oh, I want that to happen too!'' The pastor shook his head uncomprehendingly and turned away muttering to himself, ''We'll have to do something.'' That night when Paul drew near to the meeting place he saw a huge banner suspended outside the front of the hall, which read: THIS IS A PENTECOSTAL REVIVAL and underneath was written: ENTER AT YOUR OWN RISK!

There was another large church in California where Paul was invited to preach whose pastor was in the process of building a megachurch. During the meetings, however, every time Paul sensed the anointing of God's Spirit upon him, a particular woman in the congregation would interrupt him with some ecstatic utterance. Paul bore it patiently a couple of times, as his New Testament namesake had put up with the slave girl's interruptions in Acts 16, but after the third and then the fourth time, he rebuked her publicly. When she did it yet again Paul warned her: ''All right sister, if you do that once more I will expose you!'' Paul returned to his theme again and was no sooner off in full rhetorical flight when she interrupted yet again. This time Paul said: ''Lady, don't do that. You are an unclean vessel. You must not minister in these gatherings. You are living in adultery,'' and he included further details to convince her that this was no guess.

The pastor of the church closed the meeting forthwith and announced that the rest of the week's program for which Paul was billed to speak was canceled. This had never happened to Paul before and he asked the pastor why he had done it. ''Because you have lost your burden for souls,'' came the reply.

Sensing that he needed to double-check that the pastor really meant what he had said (since Paul heard the Lord telling him it was a lie), Paul asked him point blank, "Is that the real reason? Are you sure of that?" "Yes," replied the pastor, "that is the only reason." "Oh!" said Paul, "I wish you had not said that because the real reason is that that woman is married to a millionaire in your congregation who is giving you three million dollars to build your new church. That is why you are closing down my ministry here." "That's a lie," snapped the pastor angrily. "Oh!" said Paul, beginning to weep, "I just wish you had not said that as the Lord has told me that now you will never live to preach in that new church building."

Then it was the pastor's turn to weep. He begged Paul to take back that awful word. "If you withdraw I will invite you back to my new church often and you can have some great ministry there," he said. As Paul was telling the story he said that it gave him no satisfaction at all to say this, but the day the new church was finally opened the pastor was in the vestry before the service when he collapsed of a heart attack from which he never recovered.

Wherever Paul was invited, God's blessing was clearly evident. He found that by spending all the day in prayer God would give him picture after picture of people and their illnesses and many other particulars about them, such as where they would be seated and how they would be dressed and so on. Paul saw cancers shrivel and fall off and the dead raised. While he was still only eighteen, his biography had been published telling story after story of the power of God to heal and to save. Paul shudders today at the very idea of a book on his life when he had seen so very little of it, but worse still, he deplores the possibility of readers attributing any glory to him when it must all belong to the Lord!

First Public Humiliation

Paul discovered that other healing evangelists did not spend nearly as much time in prayer as he did and neither did they fast but would go out to meals with friends while engaged on their missions. Paul's custom was to spend several hours a day shut up with the Lord waiting for his message and seeking to "know" who the Lord wanted to minister to in particular. His desire for the presence of the Lord was so intense that he would sometimes ask his helpers to lock him into his closet of prayer, where he could be alone with the Lord all day. He would blindfold himself on the way to the services so that he could not see anything to distract him from the visions the Lord had so clearly given him.

One day he convinced himself that he really need not take this thing so seriously and that it must be a gift that he had been born with. He decided that he should behave a little more sociably, like other evangelists when they conducted their meetings. He went to his tent service as usual and the Lord showed him a lady who was in need of prayer. He began by describing her symptoms and was about to tell her her name, as he had done so often in the past, when his mind went completely blank. "Oh!" he cried out. "I have sinned before the Lord. The anointing has lifted from me. I cannot pray for any more tonight. I must go back to my room and repent." He left thousands of people behind him in the middle of the meeting and could not return until the following evening when it was all sorted out with the Lord again.

Paul Cain was one of the first healing evangelists to go on television. In 1952 he began to film his miracle services and these were shown weekly on secular TV stations. A businessman had fallen in love with Paul's ministry and bought him what had been the world's largest tent in those days. It would seat eight thousand people and was soon extended to seat twelve thousand. (He had bought it from another healing evangelist named Jack Coe, who was having an even bigger tent made for his meetings.)

On one occasion Paul found himself greatly troubled by a woman who followed him from meeting to meeting and took it upon herself to tell him, each time he preached, how stupid and ridiculous he was. He was really perplexed to know how to deal with this. After prayer he felt he should preach a sermon on the sins of the tongue. He made an appeal at the end of it suggesting that people might want to come forward and put their tongues (he meant it in a symbolic way) on the altar. Once again up came the woman, who assumed Paul had meant it literally and began once more to criticize him. "How ridiculous! How could I put my tongue on that altar?" she snorted sarcastically. Paul's quick wit got the better of him and before he could resist it he heard himself saying, "Well, ma'am, why don't you put on as much as you can and let the rest hang over?"

Call to Walk Alone

Paul used to go to a retreat place called Lake Sherwood, near Thousand Oaks in Southern California that belonged to a friend. This was a wonderful, quiet place where he could go to prepare himself for his meetings when he was speaking in the area. He was driving back there from San Francisco one night after a meeting, thinking of his engagement to marry a girl he had fallen in love with, when the Lord suddenly appeared beside him in the front seat of the car. He told Paul he was jealous of this particular friendship: "If you really want the kind of intimate walk with me you profess to want, you must remember that I walked alone," he said. That was not the whole substance of the conversation that seemed to last quite a little time, but it was the part Paul has felt free to share of this supernatural encounter.

Suddenly Paul became conscious of lights flashing behind him. There was certainly nothing supernatural about them! He braked as the highway patrolman flagging him down was stopping in front of him. The latter was trembling as he came back to Paul and shone his flashlight all round the interior of the car he was driving.

"Where is he?" demanded the cop in a shaky voice.

"Where's who?"

"Where is the man that was sitting in the front seat talking with you?"

"Oh!" said Paul in his Southern drawl. "That was the Lord."

"Wow!" said the patrolman, glancing strangely at Paul and then sighting his Bible on the dashboard. "Are you a minister?"

"Well yes, you could say that," Paul responded.

"Then do you realize that you and the Lord have just gone through three red lights together?" He was not joking. He was breathing heavily. "I really don't know what to do about this," he continued, thinking about his duty as a highway patrolman. "Listen, if you and the Lord will go and book up for the night in that motel up the road we'll forget the whole affair!" He muttered to himself, "Oh, Lord! How much I would like to forget this!" Once again he looked strangely at Paul and then let him go.

"Aren't you going to give me a ticket?" said Paul.

"Oh, no!" said the cop. "How could I ever give the Lord a ticket?"

Did the patrolman really accept Paul's explanation? Paul said later that he must have been a Christian cop! Who else would have believed him?

As he drew nearer to the lake where the retreat house was the Lord reappeared. Although he was fairly used to this kind of surprise by now, it was always awesome. After the Lord had finished discussing some other matters with him Paul felt it was a good opportunity to raise the question of his recent engagement to be married. So he told the Lord about it and asked: "What do you think of it, Lord?"

The Lord just looked at him kindly.

"But what do you really think about it? You don't seem very pleased. Don't you want me to be married?"

The Lord looked at him again and repeated softly, "I walked alone."

"Lord," said Paul, "if you don't want me to be married I am willing to give up the idea but you will have to do something about my feelings."

The Lord replied by simply placing his hand upon him. To Paul it felt as though fire passed right through his body. From that day to this, he says, he has never experienced any further sexual desire. That was Paul's initiation into celibacy.

Walking alone has had other problems, however. A prophet is frequently rejected and needs encouragement. When Paul refers to the "cruel essence of loneliness" it is clear he knows what he is talking about. It is something he has had to endure for long years. In an address he lamented our sick society that assumes that everyone who has chosen or been called to celibacy by the Lord is judged by the world to be "gay" and even suspected of it by other Christians. "There seems to be no place," he says, "for a Protestant celibate. Catholics understand it and are much more accepting."

Renouncing Fortunes

His calling to a single lifestyle was further tested when his friend, a former president of the National Bankers' Life Insurance, offered to share with Paul half his fortune. He was a very wealthy man and had provided Paul with his twelve-thousand-person tent. But there was one condition with which Paul could never comply. He refused the fortune.

And that was not the only time Paul had to do such a thing. On another occasion he ministered healing to Mary Virginia, a prominent member of a famous wealthy family, who had broken her back in an accident. When she died some years later she left her personal fortune to him along with that of her lately deceased brother. But the Lord told Paul not to take any of it or he would lose his anointing. This was the second fortune that Paul renounced.

On yet another occasion a wealthy Californian judge who had made a fortune out of oil asked Paul to stay at his bedside as he died. The man was horribly demonized and death was a most frightening ordeal for him. Paul agreed to visit him and the judge offered to leave Paul several million dollars—not such a large fortune as the others but more than enough for Paul. It was well known that the judge had hired a sorcerer to find the oil which made him so rich. The Lord told Paul that this money was unclean and would cause him great problems if he touched it. Telling these stories years later Paul says he had never had occasion to regret the Lord's restrictions upon him.

In 1954 Paul began planning to publish a magazine for an extensive readership. This would also serve to promote his work and the making of more films like *The Beginning of the End,* which he had made in 1954 and had proved so successful—even for church-planting in South America.

Call to Europe

News of the great blessings on Paul's ministry was being heard abroad, and wherever he held meetings great crowds showed up. Besides a tent for the congregation and a prayer tent, Paul had a tent for invalids with often a large number of stretcher and wheelchair cases brought in for healing. Hundreds would be miraculously healed. On one particular day, when Paul was ministering with Jack Coe, they prayed for over 2,000 individual cases. People walked out of their wheelchairs, were healed of their cancers, received their sight, and were delivered of demons. There were healings of all kinds. Paul also worked with Demos Shakarian, the founder of the Full Gospel Business Men's Fellowship. Often during the night Paul would see visions of the people God was going to heal the next day. On one occasion he "saw" a couple steal into a hospital and kidnap their own child, a crippled polio victim, to bring to the meeting. The Lord showed him where they would be sitting in the tent the next day; and as had so often been the case before, when he got to the tent he saw them there just as he had seen them in the vision. Paul singled out the couple, and described to them how they had "kidnapped" their own child from the hospital to bring to the meeting; before their very eyes the crippled leg was straightened out to match the other through the power of the Lord.

He tells the story of how on one occasion he wanted to buy a car. A salesman took Paul for a drive and asked him what kind of a minister he was. When Paul said that he was a Christian minister the salesman shrugged. "I hope you are not like those healers on TV," he said. By way of reply Paul simply repeated a conversation the salesman had very recently had with his wife in private. The man paled and became very serious. "You probably already know this then, but the transmission is out on this car. In fact none of the cars in this lot is any good. Don't buy any of them!"

By 1957 Paul was beginning to sense strongly that the Lord was going to call him to minister in Europe and was concerned about how the fares would be paid. He had never traveled abroad before. He was booked to minister in Washington and had decided (without apparently seeking the Lord about it) that he would ask for the offering at the biggest meeting and put that aside for his travel expenses to Europe.

Without knowing anything about this, his mother came to him and told him she did not think he should take that offering, that the Lord would send him around the world and he wouldn't need a penny. He was a little peeved over that because he thought his mother would not know about his call to Europe and how the expenses for this were weighing on his mind. But since this appeared to have been supernaturally revealed to her from the Lord, he decided not to take the offering.

Shortly after, he had a call from William Branham telling him that he had been booked to go around Europe ministering but now could not meet the commitment. (In fact Branham had actually sensed the Lord telling him not to go but to send Paul in his place.)

"Would you, Little Brother, go in my place?"

Paul felt very honored but inquired anxiously, "What shall I do about the money? I don't have any!"

"Don't worry about that, Little Brother, you won't need a penny. Your way will be paid around the world. All your expenses will be paid." These were the same words the Lord gave Paul's mother.

Paul was taken to Switzerland, then to Germany. The meetings at Karlsruhe were sponsored by the Lutheran Church and were attended by more than 30,000 a night during one week. At one of those services more than 1,500 people received Christ. The mayor of Karlsruhe sponsored over 1,000 from the Russian zone who attended nightly.

THE ALMOST SILENT YEARS

S adly, such invitations from William Branham caused jealousy among older men in the healing ministry, which brought out strong feelings of rejection in Paul. The envy surprised, shocked, and sickened the tender spirit of the young evangelist. A kind of rat race had built up around this ministry. He felt the Lord saying to him he was not to be swept into it. "Remember if you win that race you are still only a rat!"

Too many of his fellow healing evangelists were pushing too hard for visibility. This is one of the hazards of independent ministries that need a lot of money simply to keep them on the road (like some of the American televangelists of today). Money and fame were beginning to take their toll. When individual ministries of this kind were threatened there could be a lot of very unchristian backbiting. Paul was beginning to discover what it was like to be the victim of that kind of thing and confesses that he also became critical of those who criticized him.

A New Breed

Some evangelists were even falling into immorality. The Lord spoke to him very clearly one night and told him to get out of that rat race. He said, "I am going to take you aside into the desert until a new breed of men is raised up. In the days to come this ministry will be taken forward without superstars."

He then gave Paul a token promise telling him that his mother would not die till he had stood before this new breed of leaders— men and women who have learned the lessons of the past and will become an army (Joel's army, he called them). These leaders will not love the world, "the lust of the flesh, the lust of the eyes, and the pride of life" (1 John 2:16). They will not love what the Kansas City prophets call the three *g*'s: "the girls, the gold, and the glory!" They will have learned the lesson and will not bring the ministry into disrepute by falling prey to any of these common temptations.

Paul had become increasingly concerned about the direction his own ministry was taking him. The young boy who had heard the audible voice of the Lord was forgetting the wise counsel that his mother had given him: "Son, be as little as you can be and let God be as big as he can be." The personal nature of his ministry which he had once enjoyed so much had vanished. The hundreds of letters he was receiving from needy people had to be attended to by others. Paul had no time even to read most of them, let alone to pray for those who sent them. A standard form had been prepared by way of a reply. Paul Cain says he had become so "big" and was in such demand and drove himself so hard that he had no time to spend with the Lord as he had been so careful to ensure in earlier days.

The crowds were there; the finances were there; glamour and prestige were there; but the voice he had once heard so clearly had grown dull. The telephone was ringing day and night with calls from all over the nation. They all wanted to talk to the "healer." They all wanted Paul's prayers and revelations from God about their situation or condition. His phone had to be taken out and Paul had to make himself scarce. He was "too important" to take phone calls—too busy to make personal visits to pray for the dying.

Lean Times

Paul was aware that all was not well with his soul. He had lost that intimate relationship he had once so much delighted in with the Lord. But how could he get off the bandwagon while traveling at such speed? One day when plans were being made to publish an even greater magazine which would serve more than ever to get the name of Paul Cain before the people and to keep the finances going for his ministry, a crisis suddenly arose. He was stricken with a near-fatal disease that put his whole ministry in financial jeopardy, causing him to lose all the station wagons, trucks, cars, and equipment that went with his traveling tent ministry. Soon his television program was taken off the air and the magazine planned for expansion simply folded up.

The months of agony and pain were, however, a blessing in disguise. He learned what it was to be lonely again and what it felt like to be told by the doctors that his illness was terminal. He must be prepared to die. He also learned fresh lessons of the Lord's mercy and goodness. The Lord had taken him into the desert of loneliness to give him the opportunity of examining his life and ministry and restoring that intimate fellowship he had once so much enjoyed with the Lord. He felt a new longing to get back into that early habit of soaking himself in the Word of God and a ministry that exalted Christ rather than man. He so much wanted to return to that simple walk of faith, being led step by step by the spirit of God to meet the Lord's appointments. He needed to make the ministry of love his highest priority. "Though I have all faith," wrote his great namesake—words he knew so well, "so that I could remove mountains, but have not love, I am nothing" (1 Cor. 13:2). Then he remembered what the Lord had so often said to him: "Paul, I never called you to be famous; I called you to be obedient."

Like Evan Roberts of Welsh Revival fame who simply disappeared from the scene (*c.* 1907), Paul renounced everything. He went back to his home in Phoenix, Arizona, to look after his aging mother with the help of a married sister living nearby. He destroyed his collection of newspaper cuttings which reported so many of the signs and wonders he had witnessed. Away went all the testimonies of conversion and healing which he had been involved in during the brief years of his public ministry. Now his still youthful heart yearned for holiness because he knew that that was what the Lord was yearning for him. Paul Cain had to learn holiness the hard way, just as everyone who seeks to be holy does. A little girl once prayed with simple insight and feeling: "Lord make the bad people good and the good people nice." She had something there. Not everyone found Paul's holy life easy to take.

The Jesus People

In the 1970s California saw a remarkable ministry among the hippies which became known as the Jesus People Movement. Paul was invited to help and was eager to assist in whatever way he could. He was asked to pick up a musical group of recently converted hippies who would be participating in the meeting where he was to speak. He packed them into his mobile home—a sacred vehicle with every part of it prayed over by Paul and dedicated to the Lord. The vehicle was undefiled by drink, smoking, drugs, sexual impurity, or foul language of any kind. Paul was horrified to find these Christian hippies drinking, smoking, and possibly taking drugs, while appearing totally insensitive to other people's feelings or possessions. They dropped half-empty beer cans on the floor and their stubbed-out cigarettes littered the interior; they dropped half-eaten food on the carpet and one of them even scratched the glove compartment in striking a match. Paul was inwardly furious and would gladly have murdered one of them, but he knew he had to forgive.

Eventually they reached the meeting place where the Jesus People were to play their part with Paul. As the meeting was drawing to its close, Paul sensed the Lord saying that when the crowd gathered again the next day they would witness the incredible healing of a brain-damaged cripple. Paul was just about to say this when one of the team gave out an identical invitation! And so it was! The cripple's name was Brian and he was miraculously healed, even going up on the stage to play a musical instrument to prove it. The miracle was incredible indeed, but what was more incredible to Paul was that the Lord should have used such uncouth youths to do this. It softened his heart and grace was given for a great reconciliation between them all. The young men confessed to him that they had found his "holiness" obnoxious but then they apologized for going too far in their reaction to it. It was another lesson that Paul had the grace to learn.

Unnecessary Overkill

Sometimes, these days, Paul thinks there may have been a little unnecessary overkill in his earnest pursuit after holiness. He regrets some of his hastiness in destroying all those archives. Perhaps in his old age they would have revived treasured memories for him of the power and glory of God. But God knew his motives—those of a rare species of Christian—unusual especially in one so much and so early in the public eye. Paul thirsted with holy zeal after righteousness; no sacrifice or discipline was too much. He readily embraced the wilderness life for nearly thirty years.

Paul published an article in the late 1950s describing his reflections on his own experiences of the healing ministry and the way the Lord had led him since. This article was carried by many religious periodicals of the day. He received some 5,000 letters about it, and it was republished several times. Many of Paul's contemporary healing-evangelists considered this a betrayal and reacted unkindly to him. But the article proved to be the knife which severed Paul completely from the past and set him free to walk in humility and obedience until God was ready to use him again.

Recently God has been reminding him that he has not forgotten the call which is still upon his life. Paul Cain believes that God has shown him that in the last days there is to be a restoration of revelatory prophecy to the church. He sees this as sharing the visions and messages that God has given him with accompanying signs to inspire a new order of prophets. These would spur on the church to follow after holiness. They will not dare to touch the glory that belongs to the Lord, and they will encourage the faithful to create new wineskins for the revival which is imminent.

'End Times' Outpourings

He quotes Joel's prophecy to which Peter likens the manifestation of the Spirit at Pentecost. The prophecy of Joel still awaits the complete fulfillment promised for the last days when:

> I will pour out My Spirit on all flesh; your sons and your daughters shall prophesy, your old men shall dream dreams, your young men shall see visions; and also on My menservants and on My maidservants I will pour out My Spirit in those days. And I will show wonders in the heavens and in the earth: blood and fire and pillars of smoke. The sun shall be turned into darkness, and the moon into blood, before the coming of the great and terrible day of the LORD (Joel 2:28–31).

Paul gives a kind of mini-model of this in his public meetings. Having foretold what God intends to do for and through an individual person, the Church, or the nation, Paul will then give a token sign; he will call out someone, usually until that moment completely unknown to him, and then reveal details about that person, some well known and some that only the individual concerned, or a very limited number of people, could possibly know. Frequently he will identify some ailment—diabetes, cancer, a heart condition, a growth or some other illness—and speak healing in Jesus' name.

A Sign We Checked Out Ourselves

An acquaintance of ours named Debbie, who works in the Vineyard Christian Fellowship at Anaheim in California and whom we and some of our church members have known for several years, had been married for nearly a decade and all that time she had been wanting and praying for a baby. In spite of all the medical attention and the prayers she had been unable to conceive. She was in Kansas City a short while ago when Paul Cain was ministering at the Olathe Worship Center, one of the five new centers that have grown out of the original Kansas City Fellowship.

Though neither had met the other before, he identified her by name in a public meeting as someone who was praying for a baby but could not conceive. He told her that God had heard her prayers and that she would conceive that very week. When I met her later she told me she had indeed conceived that week and was by then several months pregnant. For her this was a veritable miracle. It was also a sign that Paul's prophecy should be taken seriously.

Power Surges

Mike Bickle told me of a particular night that week when Paul had been prophesying and the power of God came down mightily.

Everyone began to sense the "manifest presence of God" power-fully in the room. Mike was speechless. A spirit of great boldness came upon Paul and he reeled off about seven names in rapid succession with accompanying words of knowledge, all of which were incredibly accurate. There were many spontaneous healings and miracles and much revelatory information during sixty to ninety intense, power-packed seconds. People were gasping in amazement and giving glory to God. A solemn awe fell over the whole place. Some simply remained sitting still in their seats. Others tiptoed the aisles in trembling silence.

Suddenly there was the sound of sirens as two fire engines screeched to a standstill right outside the center. The doors burst open and a number of uniformed firemen with hoses and axes demanded to know where the fire was. Mike shook his head, hardly able to cope with such an abrupt and earthly "landing."

"There is no fire here," he said.

"Oh, yes, there's a big one somewhere! Down at the station all the signals possible are going for this place. The circuits have blown and set off the alarm system. There are signs of a tremendous power surge," said the leading fireman, hardly waiting in his frenzied rush to find the fire.

They hunted high and low, of course, as their professionalism dictated. No fire could they find anywhere! Not even a whiff of smoke! And no one in the packed building had panicked. The firemen left completely mystified.

After the meeting Paul turned quietly to Mike and apologized. "I am so sorry about the fire scare. I should have warned you that that does sometimes happen when there is a lot of divine power about!"

On his first visit to Anaheim in February 1988 Paul saw power-ful lights across the room and a strong sense of the presence of God was accompanied by revelations in the word of knowledge. On that occasion an expensive video camera was short-circuited.

This was battery operated and not plugged into any outlet. The next night the telephone system was blown out though no one was on the phone at the time.

Paul Cain has been more or less a recluse in his home for the past twenty-seven years except for the times he has been sent to warn a religious or political leader of something God had revealed to him. Other exceptions have been occasionally when he sensed the Lord's leading to speak in a church or at a conference somewhere, where people were ready to experience a Pentecostal visitation once more. Instead of two hundred to two hundred fifty engagements a year Paul would now go out some four to eight times and only then on guarantee that there would be none of the kind of promotion or publicity which had attended his earlier ministry.

Restoration of Prophetic Office

A couple of years ago Paul received a word from the Lord that he was to visit several evangelical leaders of significance in the U.S. and some beyond. He took a message from the Lord to each of them. He found the responses varied—some listened and some rejected his words. Paul was seeking a leader with the anointing of God upon him, whom God had prepared to respond in a certain way.

Like Samuel with Jesse's sons, after each meeting he had to inquire if there was not yet one more. He had visited a number of Christian leaders and had almost exhausted the list of those he could think of. But though he felt his health was a continuing problem which limited him seriously, he never gave up the search.

NEW CHURCH IN KANSAS CITY

A s the reader is aware, we first met Paul Cain through Mike Bickle. It was he who first shared with us both the great blessing of having a prophet of the Lord in the local church and a constructive approach to the raising of a prophetic ministry. This approach will be developed in more detail later (chapter 11).

A Young Leader

Mike Bickle was the leader of the thriving Kansas City Fellowship but he seemed very young to be heading such a large gifted team—about twenty-five church-planters, prophets, teachers, pastors, and administrators. Besides his responsibilities as leader, preacher, and teacher, the major part of his time (like that of the New Testament apostles) was given over to prayer and study of the Bible. He was married in 1977 to Diane (née Marion) and has two sons, Luke, age eleven, and Paul, nine. His father, Robert Bickle, had been a world champion amateur boxer (welter-weight) in the 1950s. Mike had grown up in the champion's home in Kansas City where he had been educated initially, and then had gone to Washington to study medicine.

As far as his church background goes he had once been a

Catholic and later a Presbyterian. In his late teens he had had a personal experience of conversion to Christ. That was in 1971.

A school friend, David Parker, now on the staff of KCF, still remembers the impact of Mike's conversion on his fellow students. Mike, like his father who had doubtlessly contributed to his training as an athlete, was well built and fully committed to a number of athletic programs. At the school there seemed to be some kind of a division between the committed athletes and the leather-jacketed "greasers." Every now and then the latter would seek to provoke a fight between the groups if they knew they were beyond the eagle eye of the school authorities. The first time this happened after Mike's conversion, the athletes looked to him for their cue. He would normally have responded to the challenge with considerable gusto. But Mike seemed to have something else in mind. The leader of the greasers took a step forward and held up his fist to him menacingly. "No!" said Mike. "I won't fight you because Jesus Christ has told me to love you!" Once again the greaser shook his fist. "No!" Mike repeated without moving, whereupon the greaser landed him a punch in the face. Mike still did nothing but looked straight at him. It was a tense moment because the athletes knew it was in Mike's power to trounce him at that game. When it was obvious that Mike was not going to respond in kind the leader landed him another. "No," said Mike, "I won't strike you—I love you for Christ's sake." It was too much for the gang. They quickly dispersed and their leader, seeing he was almost isolated, strutted away in assumed disgust to hide his shame. It was a telling act of Christian witness. The marks and bruises on Mike's face healed but the impact on his classmates lasted a long time.

Today his five sisters and their husbands all worship at the Kansas City Fellowship, as does Pat, his younger brother, who is paraplegic. Soon after his commitment to Christ, Mike developed a great passion for the Bible. His vast knowledge of the Word of God is widely commented on by all who know him. A mutual friend said he thought it could be the result of Bickle's long-practiced habit of turning the Scriptures back into prayer to God.

A Call to Full-time Ministry

This knowledge and love of the Bible was so marked that he was invited to leave college at twenty and minister full time to a small group of Bible-loving Christians in St. Louis, Missouri. A partner in his ministry there was his friend Bob Scott, who continues to work alongside him today as the administrator of the Kansas City Fellowship.

While still at college his father had visited him and talked over the problem of his brother Pat. In 1973, as a teenager, Pat had suffered a broken neck playing high school football. Being the son of a father made famous through sport, the story of the tragedy had been front-page news in the Kansas City press. In a radio interview following the accident Pat had bravely shared his faith saying: "God will deliver me one day!" For the family there was now the question of who was going to have the long-term responsibility of looking after Pat in his paralyzed condition.

Mike's father had come specifically to ask Mike to promise he would take on that responsibility should anything happen to him. It is not clear whether Mike had any inkling at that time of his father's terminal heart condition, but his father died soon after. At least he had died with one consolation: the assurance he had so badly wanted from his eldest son regarding the future care of Pat.

Since the beginning Pat has believed that God would heal him one day. The heavy responsibility for Pat so willingly taken up was one of the factors which had led Mike to develop his marked discipline for intercession. This in turn has become a distinctive characteristic of the Kansas City Fellowship. There are three two-hour sessions for intercessory prayer there every day.

Mike had been away from Kansas City for just seven years when he was led back in June 1982 through remarkable circumstances. While still pastoring a church with a membership of over four hundred in St. Louis, Missouri, he had his first encounter with a prophet whose name was Agustine Alcala.

An Unknown Prophet

Agustine was driving past a church one Thursday evening (it happened to be the one under Mike's leadership but of that Agustine knew absolutely nothing), when the Lord suddenly gave him a powerful prophecy for the pastor there. Since he did not know who this was, Agustine drove to a friend in town and inquired who the pastor of that particular church would be. Did his friend know the man? Yes, indeed he did! The friend told him the pastor was a gifted young man named Mike Bickle.

Agustine then explained that he had a message from the Lord for Mike and would like to speak to him urgently, so this friend called him up on the telephone. "Hello Mike, I have got a prophet here who has a word straight from the Lord for you. Will you speak with him?" A prophet was really the last thing Mike felt like talking to at that moment. "That's all I need," said Mike to himself, "a prophet!" Frantic thoughts of how to handle such a strange phenomenon were racing through his mind. However should he answer this one, he wondered? Politely and as definitely as he could he replied, "I appreciate your call but thanks—not just now!" and put down the receiver. Mike's later comment was, "He didn't tell me it was an audible voice he had heard from God—but then I would not have believed him anyway!"

The Prophet Goes to Church

Agustine then decided he would have to visit the church and see the man himself so he went there and took a seat in the front row. He happened to choose one of those Sundays when for a number of reasons Mike arrived late and slipped quietly into the sound-control booth at the back, unseen by the congregation facing the front. The service was being led by another brother somewhat older than Mike. Some three hundred to four hundred people were engaged in worship there that morning.

Suddenly Agustine summoned the courage to stand up and introduce himself (something Mike would never allow to happen in his church today). He began, "Hello! I'm Agustine—the Lord uses me to speak prophetically." And prophetically he spoke without more ado! At the back Mike was thinking, "Oh my, those are pretty bold statements!" But Mike was intrigued by it all, not least because he recognized the truth of what the stranger was saying. "Perhaps someone has been telling him things about us," thought Mike, who just could not make it out. He was viewing it all with caution: "Maybe yes and maybe no," he mused.

Then the prophet began to call out three or four people Mike knew well and was telling them things which he realized the prophet just could not have known naturally. He was beginning to admit to himself that he was impressed. Suddenly the prophet turned about to address Mike directly where he was still sitting above the congregation level in the sound-control booth at the back.

Riddle of the Pastor's Identity

The prophet, of course, had no idea that the man he was pointing at was the pastor. In fact he was still quite confused about that because he assumed the older man up front was the pastor—

58

and yet he had been told by his friend that the pastor was a young man! And neither the man up front nor Mike at the back was wearing anything which could distinguish them as ministers—so it really was very confusing for Agustine.

"That young man at the back of the room!"

"Me?" asked Mike.

"Yes, you," said the prophet, pointing directly at him.

By this time Mike was totally embarrassed. Everyone, of course, knew who he was except the prophet, who continued, "Young man, the Lord has called you into the ministry and he is going to redirect your path into something completely new."

When he had finished a handful clapped and others muttered protests *sotto voce:* Whoever did this man think he was? And didn't he know that he was speaking to their pastor? How dare he address him publicly as "that young man"!

Someone asked Mike later if his spirit had witnessed in any way to the prophecy. Mike replied that he had been so confused that he would have to listen to the tape-recorded service afterwards to find out what it was all about!

At the end of the service the prophet made his way towards Mike still not knowing who he was. "Hey, why don't you come out to eat with me so that I can get to know you?" he said. "The Lord has certainly got some powerful things in store for you to do. I'm trying to get to the pastor so that I can invite him out too."

Mike agreed and when the prophet had found the older man he thought was the pastor they set off together. It was not till they reached the restaurant that it dawned on Agustine who the pastor he was looking for really was!

A Message He Did Not Want

That was more or less how Mike and Agustine first crossed paths personally. But Mike was not about to be taken in; besides, he had been very happy in St. Louis and was not wanting to leave at all. He had no idea what he was meant to do now about the strange message Agustine was pressing on him.

"I heard the audible voice of the Lord," insisted Agustine. "This is a very serious word from God!"

Mike played at being vague: First, he did not know what to think about audible voices! Second, he did not know what to think about prophecies! And third, he did not know anything about this kind of thing at all!

"It's all so completely new to me!" he replied, trying to get the message across that he was not a person to be easily duped.

A week later Mike was visiting relatives in Kansas City, planning on staying there for a few days. This was after he had decided with the elders in St. Louis that they would have to discuss the prophecy together sometime when he got back. Talking to a minister friend at the Presbyterian church, he and his wife were suddenly asked, right out of the blue, how long they thought they would be staying at St. Louis. Mike's wife Diane replied for herself, saying, "For the rest of our lives! What do you think, Mike?"

"I can never see us leaving St. Louis," said Mike. "We just love it there so much."

Famous last words!

That was on Tuesday. Then on Wednesday the Lord spoke to Mike in a very unusual and dramatic way. He was told quite clearly that he was to move to Kansas City! In spite of such remarkable confirmation Mike really did not know how to proceed from there.

Egyptian Retreat

Soon after this, Mike had to fulfill another long-standing commitment to join a team of eight North American pastors conducting teaching conferences across India. At the end of that time the other American pastors flew off east. Mike's own travels led him through Egypt, where he had a visitation from the spirit of the Lord while kneeling in prayer on the floor of his hotel room in Cairo. God then spoke to him in an internal voice—it was so clear that he said he could even hear the intonations of it.

The Lord's word to Mike was: "I am inviting you to be a part of a work that will reach to the ends of the earth." On hearing this a great fear fell upon Mike and he began to weep before the Lord and a spirit of groaning and travail welled up in him.

The voice continued: "I have invited many people to do this thing and many have said yes." Mike was sobbing as he heard himself responding, "Yes, Lord, yes!" The Lord impressed upon him that it was simply not enough to say yes. Too many had said just that. There must be a commitment to obedience.

Then he heard the Lord say, "This is very serious," and he outlined to him how the work would be accomplished.

"First, it will be built on night and day prayer.

"Second, it will be built upon holiness of heart.

"Third, it will be built upon unwavering faith.

"Finally, it will be built upon extravagant giving to the poor.

"Besides the Lord Jesus himself, these four principles will be the foundations of this work."

Mike was still weeping and saying, "Oh, Lord—yes—yes!"

The Lord continued: "Guard your heart, for if you lose this vision it will be your brothers who have stolen it from you—it will not be the world that does that. It will be reasoning brothers who do not know my ways that will try to take this thing from your heart. Guard your heart lest your brothers steal this from you. If this standard is upheld, which I am inviting you and your people to follow, you will fulfill a purpose that will touch the ends of the earth."

It was not just the fact of the visitation; it was the magnitude of the vision and the standards of it that left Mike astounded. He has said that many times since then, numbers of well-meaning people of Christ, who have professed to be trying to help in the work, have assaulted and resisted those standards. Many good people have wagged their fingers at Mike, saying "You are out of your mind!" and have left the fellowship. Mike has learned—the hard way—to understand what the Lord meant when he said, "Guard your heart."

The word from the Lord had been crystal clear. These God-given principles have since become completely nonnegotiable as far as Mike is concerned. He says he will not even discuss them after that solemn warning to guard his heart.

Further Confirmation

They returned to St. Louis and for three months remained sitting quietly and simply waiting. At last, in September, Mike got around to sharing it with the elders. They were a little confused but they had all heard, or heard about, Agustine's prophecy and felt that with such clear confirmation it must indeed be God calling after all.

So very soon after, in obedience to this strange and strong call, Mike and Diane, their friend Bob Scott, and a few others, all packed up and went to plant a new church in Kansas City. In their prayers together they felt they should ask for a building in the south of Kansas City, one that would seat seven hundred people. Their search seemed frenzied and frustrating. They managed to look at twenty-eight places in four months but it appeared there were no such buildings available to them: nobody would believe they could raise the necessary rent. When it came to the interview with the agents the dialogue soon became all too familiar and the outcome almost predictable.

"How many church members do you have?" the agent would ask.

"Hm, well, we've got about eight people in total committed to this," Mike would reply.

Roars of laughter all around followed as the agent closed his book, bringing another interview to its fruitless conclusion.

A Building at Last

Then at last they found someone who owned a suitable building and was willing to trust them. Without further ado Mike signed the contract. He was told he would need to put down $21,000 by Wednesday.

"No problem," Mike heard himself saying. "We can get that all right." He was thinking, "I will have to get Bob Scott to sort that out—he's always so good at finances!"

He went off and found Bob Scott.

"We've got a place at last!" said Mike enthusiastically.

"Have you? How much?" was Bob's immediate reply.

"Bob, why all this concern about detail?"

"How much?" demanded Bob insistently.

"The rent is $8,000 a month. But don't worry! I am sure we'll soon get that together somehow," said Mike.

"Yeah!" said Bob, looking resigned.

"One other thing though, Bob! We need $21,000 advance payment by Wednesday!"

There were five days in which to find it.

Now for the Money

They had no idea where it could possibly come from. Only the Lord knew and the eight of them went to him once more in prayer. They had committed themselves not to tell a single soul of their financial needs. It was so vital to have the Lord's seal on this venture. They all felt that either the Lord was going to destroy this thing outright or he was going to make it come to pass by providing the money.

Amazingly, two different people came to visit them, having heard they were wanting to rent premises to start a church in town. They said they wanted to help. Between them they gave $20,000. By then it was Tuesday afternoon.

That night Mike had to fulfill a long-standing engagement to speak at a meeting in St. Louis. He flew there and gave the address. Afterwards the treasurer approached him, saying, "We do not normally give our speakers anything except their expenses and a little extra. We do not know why but we have a strong impression that the Lord is telling us to give you a thousand dollars." They had known nothing about the urgent need of exactly that sum. The Lord had marvelously provided. Mike was excited as he returned to Kansas City giving glory to God.

Agustine Again

It seemed that no sooner had Mike returned to Kansas City than Agustine was back in town. It was still September 1982.

"Are you going to go ahead with planting this new church?" he asked Mike.

"Yeah," said Mike with a nod of his head.

"Okay," said Agustine. "Then the Lord has told me four things you are to hide in your heart which will be very important for you. The first two are really glorious and the second two are terrible!

"One, multitudes of young people—thousands will be rallied to you."

Mike nodded, "That sounds great! What's the second?"

"Two, in the days to come there will be a full manifestation of the gifts of the spirit but it will be for an appointed time."

"That sounds great too! What's the third?"

Agustine continued: "Three, there will be a false prophet in your midst from the very beginning. If you are patient and discern him you will save the church great heartache. If you do not you will suffer many, many problems.

"Four, finally there will be resistance and misunderstanding. Do not lose heart."

Starting with Prayer

Mike had started the new fellowship by summoning the little group together for regular prayer. They prayed every night for three hours from 7:00 to 10:00 P.M.; and they continued like that for two years.

In January 1983 an excited Christian brother bounced up to Mike, saying, "Hey! There's a prophet by the name of Bob Jones in Kansas City. He's been talking for ten years about a group of people the Lord had told him were coming to the south of Kansas City who would be led by a twenty-seven-year-old man. [That was Mike's age at the time.] The group would speak about intercession and revival. [That was exactly what Mike was teaching on.] Your group is the group God has told him about and he wants to come and see you."

Immediately all the warning bells about the false prophets began to ring and Mike responded: "No! I'm not interested in meeting him. Maybe some other time."

A month or two later up came another brother well known to Mike Bickle and said, "Hey! You must meet this guy Bob Jones. I've known him for years. He said that our group is the one the Lord has told him about and he very much wants to meet with you for just a short time."

Mike felt that the sooner he could sort this "false prophet" business out the better and this time reluctantly agreed to see him.

Enter Bob Jones

It was March 7, 1983, when Bob Jones eventually got his foot through the door of Mike's office. Bob looked older than his fifty-three years. As he entered he was obviously sensing some kind of anointing from God in his hands.

"Uhuh! Uhuh!" he muttered to himself and then looked up, "Yeah! This is the group. I've seen you!"

Not properly understanding what Bob was saying and not wanting any "false prophet" to get one up on him, Mike replied quickly, "Yeah! I've seen you too," thinking of Agustine's serious warning.

"I thought you probably had," murmured Bob with disarming pleasantness. But he obviously had not understood what Mike was meaning either, in his excitement to meet the young man at last.

And Mike was soon finding it hard to understand what Bob was meaning too.

"I have come to get involved with a purpose of God," he said, "which is going to become worldwide, which is going to touch the nations of the earth with such power and glory that it will go far beyond the book of Acts!"

Mike was startled. "What purpose?" he stammered quietly, quickly running through all the implications of this in his mind.

"Yeah! The Lord told me that you would not know anything about that yet. My first task is to get you to believe it because the sooner you do the more difficulties you will avoid."

Bob began to relate a strange vision involving a white horse, which at that stage Mike had great difficulty in understanding.

66

He had yet to learn that most of Bob Jones's visions were parables, and therefore somewhat enigmatic.

Foretelling His Own Acceptance

Finally Bob Jones concluded: "The Lord tells me that on the first day of spring when the snows melt we will sit around the table—and the Lord gave me the words *agape* and *koinonia*—and we will sit around the table and they will accept me!"

"Whatever is this man talking about?" Mike thought, and then aloud he asked, "Who will accept you?"

"They will," replied Bob.

"And who are 'they'?" Mike questioned.

"Well, you guys will!" said Bob.

Mike was now sure that this must be the false prophet. It was all so clear, he thought. But Bob was still rambling on.

He said, "Let me tell you again. Last September 1982—six months ago—the Lord told me that on the first day of spring when the snows begin to melt the group will finally receive me." He was obviously very earnest about being accepted.

Mike was thinking fast. The winter was already over. They were into unseasonably warm weather and everyone was saying that spring had come early. Whatever was he going on about? Anyone who prophesied his own acceptance had to be a false prophet! Mike was certain.

As Bob was leaving he turned at the door with a throwaway postscript. "Oh, by the way, the Lord has told me to tell you these four things but he said that you would already know them:

"One, thousands of young people will be rallied to you.

"Two, you will see a full manifestation of the gifts of the spirit among you.

"Three, there will be a false prophet in your midst from the beginning.

"Four, there will be major resistance to you and misunderstanding but you are not to lose heart."

"Whew!" gasped Mike, flinching on the horns of this fresh dilemma. "However could a false prophet tell me that?" It was exactly what the Lord had already told him through Agustine!

After Sunday worship for the public had commenced in October 1984, they began meeting regularly for prayer three times daily (for a total of six hours a day).

BEWARE THE FALSE PROPHET!

The first time Bob Jones came to the Kansas City Fellowship church after that strange meeting, a woman in the congregation breezed up to Mike saying, "See that guy?" pointing to Bob Jones. "He's a false prophet."

"Yeah! I know," said Mike, "I'm watching him carefully."

Later another person came up and singled out Bob.

"See that man over there? He's a false prophet."

"Yeah! Thanks!" said Mike. "I've got my tabs on that guy—don't worry!"

Without giving further details Mike said later that, unwittingly, he was in fact meeting regularly with a false prophet (he has never revealed publicly who this was) and there he was watching for an excuse to throw out a genuine one—for that is what Bob Jones turned out to be.

The Poor Farmer's Son

Bob Jones was born of humble parentage, the son of an illiterate "cotton-cuttin'" sharecropper, and raised in the 1930s among the cotton fields of Gravely, Arkansas. His spiritual nurture had been in the Baptist church there, but he had had no real spiritual experience. He was experienced in other ways and had become quite a talented thief early in life.

At about the age of nine he experienced his first supernatural visitation. Ambling along a dusty track one day he suddenly saw an angel on a white charger coming towards him. The angel stopped right before him in the middle of the track and, taking out a large silver trumpet, he put it to his lips and blew. The angel then turned, looked straight at Bob, and disappeared.

Paralyzed with fear, Bob stood transfixed where he was for quite a while before turning tail and running for home. "I thought he was calling me to die and to give up sin and I didn't want to do either," said Bob. There was no one he felt he could talk to about that experience. He never mentioned anything about it to anyone until after his conversion to Christ years later.

When he was thirteen he had a second visitation, this time in a cotton field at the time of cotton picking. He was walking along the track when he heard his name called. He did not know how he knew, but he knew it was the Lord calling him. Again he related the visitation to death, which he now realizes it was—though not quite as he imagined: rather a death to self and rising to Christ. Once more he was filled with terror and rushed for home. The call was still not welcome.

Mystical Experience

Two years later he had a further mystical experience of great significance. He was brought before the throne of God in a vision. The glory, the piercing light that went right through him and showed up in detail everything that he saw there, so terrified him that it took him about three months to recover— he shook so much. He thought that to see what he had seen he should have died and only the presence of an angel standing in front of him protecting his eyes enabled him to survive. When the vision was over he was still hurting from a burning feeling within his very bones.

He knew that what he had seen was the real thing, but he still did not realize that it was God's call upon his life—or rather he did not want to realize it. He struggled hard to forget. Striving to find peace in sin he ran away from God.

Running Away from God

When the Korean War came Bob Jones joined the U.S. Marine Corps, where he soon became involved in drunken brawls, fist-fights, and gambling. "I had no trouble at all making grades [getting promotions]," said Bob. "They sort of approved of what I did." Once a man fired at him at pointblank range but the revolver failed to go off. A fistfight ensued and he beat up his opponent. Afterwards a friend picked up the gun and fired it at the ceiling to see what was wrong with it. It went off! Bob realized that his life had been spared. In another brawl at Santa Monica every marine got hurt except Bob. He knew then that there must be someone protecting him and he was still running away from him.

All this time Bob was leading his marine companions into sin and himself into ever-deepening misery until eventually he left the corps. He and his wife, Viola, started to run an illegal liquor store in the "dry" state of Oklahoma where they made a lot of money. His dream was to buy himself a big bar in the middle of town and retire. But it all came to nothing; at thirty-nine he was worn out. Sleepless nights and a godless life had left him exhausted. His own comment in retrospect, "The damned can't rest," summed up those wearisome days.

71

Veterans' Hospital

Finally he went to a doctor who put him on drugs but could not cure him. He was facing a complete breakdown. His family had moved to Kansas City when he was still in his teens. Now he was sent to the Veterans' Hospital in Topeka nearby, where he was treated by a Christian doctor.

"I am taking you off dope," he said.

"But doctor," pleaded Bob, "I can't live without it."

"Oh, yes, you can, if you are going to live at all!" he insisted.

It seemed like hell to come off those drugs. All Bob could do was to pace the corridors of the hospital throughout the long nights. His hands were shaking continuously and involuntarily. One night his doctor saw what was happening and said, "If I tell you to do something that will stop that shaking will you do it without question?"

"Yes, sir!" said Bob eagerly.

"Come with me," he said and led Bob trembling along the corridor to the cleaning cupboard where he took out a mop. "Now," he said, "every time you shake I want you to mop the floor."

Bob began to protest, "Me, mop the floor?"

"Yes," he said, "mop the floor!"

Bob relates the story himself. "I had never done anything like that before in my life, but I found that when I began to mop the floors the shaking began to subside. I did it for days from about midnight to six o'clock in the morning."

Then a friend sent him a book on Psalm 23 and as Bob read it he realized that he was terrified of hell. He began to cry out to the Lord for help. At about three o'clock one morning he knelt beside his hospital bed and repeated the psalm. As he did so he sensed a demon at his bedside speaking to him: "Everyone has mistreated you in your life. No wonder you are like you

72

are. You deserve to get even with them. Here is a list of twelve people that are responsible for your being here. Why don't you run away tonight and kill them and then come back? You are in the crazy ward anyway and you're going to be here for the rest of your life. They won't do anything to you.''

Discharged at Last

Immediately Bob cried out, ''Help me, Lord Jesus! Help me!''

Then the Lord came to Bob and said to him, ''I can't help you Bob, until you forgive those people who have hurt you.''

So Bob proceeded to forgive them one by one and then he passed on to others the Lord was bringing to mind. He went back into the past as far as he could remember.

Then the Lord said to him, ''One of your greatest sins is self-pity. You blame everyone for your problems.''

He felt something strange beginning to happen to him. The next day he was singing and whistling! His doctor stopped him in the corridor and said, ''What's happened to you? Come and see me in my office.''

When he had heard Bob's latest news he said, ''I've just got one more little job for you. Tonight I want you to take charge of the padded cells!''

Bob said he was both surprised and disappointed as he was so looking forward to what he believed would be his first good night's sleep. But he did what the doctor told him to do. Next day he saw the doctor again, who said, ''You handled that pretty well! Now get out of this place.''

Back to Church

As the doctor discharged him he told him how he and the church he attended had been praying for him. So Bob decided to go to

73

his doctor's church and see what it was like. He found it was a Baptist church like the one he had gone to in his early childhood and he soon felt at home there. He began to read the Bible whenever he could. He wanted to cooperate with the Lord in every way possible, but he still had no assurance that his sins were forgiven. "Getting to that place where I knew I was saved was the hardest thing for me," said Bob. Every time there was a gospel call in church Bob was on his way up to the front again to get saved. He was still reading his Bible fervently, day in and day out, and finally he found peace with God.

Bob was discovering a strange thing happening to him. Whenever people were praising God in church he would find himself knowing things which he could not naturally know—not just about people and things going on in church. Once he found himself "knowing" that Patty Hearst, the famous newspaper publisher's daughter who had been abducted by a weird political group, was going to be rescued within thirty days. He shared this with the church publicly. Within thirty days Patty Hearst was in fact rescued just as he had predicted.

Disturbed by Visions

The church accepted that this was a gift which he had and at first was not at all disturbed by it, though Bob admits he was rather frightened himself. He just kept praying for protection through the blood of Jesus as he had been taught to do in the Baptist church. Visions continued to be triggered off whenever the people raised their hands in worship, spoke in tongues, or simply praised the Lord!

After Bob's "final conversion" he was baptized in a lake on August 6, 1975. Some friends then came and told him they should now lay hands on him and pray that he might be filled with the Holy Spirit. Bob was none too enthusiastic and did not really see the point. But these were good friends of his and they had arranged to take him out for a meal afterwards so he submitted to their request, as he says, "simply to pacify them."

As they laid hands on him and prayed for him something warm suddenly started running down his head and his back and then his mind began filling up with a colorful vision and he was speaking in tongues. He saw a landscape with the sun setting over it like the last hour of the day; it was impressed upon him that soon it would be too late for any man to labor in the harvest fields. He sensed the Lord telling him to pray that he would send out laborers to work in his harvest field.

Learning to Prophesy

After that baptism and the laying on of hands Bob was returning home in his truck when he felt the Lord telling him to prophesy against abortion.

"How do I do that, Lord?" asked Bob.

"Just raise your voice and speak it out," the Lord told him quite simply.

So he did just that and as he began to prophesy against abortion he could suddenly see it all happening and hear the mothers and babies screaming. Sickened by the awful horror of it Bob finished his prophecy with the words: "As you destroy the first-born and the fruit of the womb so you will be destroyed."

Not surprisingly, as he shared this with the churches he began to find himself becoming unpopular: "Don't bring these awful prophecies here," they said.

Bob was then given another prophecy—this time against homosexuality. He began calling church leaders on the phone and telling them. As he persisted a demon appeared, speaking to him face to face. The demon told him that if he kept on prophesying against abortion and homosexuality he would kill him!

75

"But I told the demon to get lost—I'm doing the Lord's work," said Bob.

The demon did not leave but changed tack with some subtle temptations until Bob picked up the phone and "reported" the demon to a praying friend telling him just what the demon was saying to him. At this the demon disappeared.

Enemy Counterattack

Shortly after this Bob and his son Robert were out spraying fruit trees (that was how Bob earned his bread and butter). On later reflection, Bob said, recounting the experience, he should have taken the devil's threat much more seriously. Five minutes after starting work he began to feel great pain from the waist down. Every muscle ached and he was gripped by violent cramps.

The pain was so bad he had to go home. When things got worse the doctor wanted to get him to the hospital but Bob protested, "No! I know what's wrong. If I am going to die I'm going to die! And if that's the case then I want to die at home!"

The doctor gave him some painkillers. Bob took two but the pain intensified. Then he started to hemorrhage from the nose and mouth. Bob wrapped a towel round his head and fell back on to his bed. Then the pain was gone. "Suddenly I was in a dark place—a cave," said Bob. "There was a crystal light at the end and I knew that it was the Lord!"

Bob thought, "So the devil did kill me after all! How could he do that?" As he started walking towards the Lord another thought began to press upon Bob: "Did I get my robe clean?" He looked to see and the robe was like crystal light. There were no spots or darkness in it. He began to cry, "I'm coming home clean after all I've been up to in my past. Oh! Thank you, Lord!"

How Could the Devil Do This to Me?

Then I asked the Lord, "How could the devil do this to me when I was busy doing your work?"

And the Lord put his hand up and said, "You go back and teach the leaders of the latter-day church the old leadership is coming to an end. A new quality of leadership across the earth with a deep commitment to the Word of God, a passion for Jesus, and a burden for holiness is coming into being to bring forth the bride of Christ."

"But Lord," persisted Bob, "how did the devil get me?"

By way of an answer several possible reasons came to mind. In the first place, he did not have the protection from others interceding on his behalf. Secondly, he did not have the covering of a local church leader. Finally, he was immature and had been rebuking the devil out of his own faith. The next thing he heard was the Lord telling him that he was sending him back!

Back into His Own Body

Bob described how he returned to the room. His body was still there wrapped in the towel. He remembered thinking to himself, "I don't want to go back into that body where I had so much pain." Then he saw two large angels that were praying for him. There was a dark angel behind them, but they would not let it touch Bob so it left. The two angels were talking about a group of young people who would be setting up in Kansas City.

"When I returned to that body I thought that I would be healed," said Bob, "but I wasn't. The pain was as bad as when I left the body."

The only relief that subsequently came was through other people's prayers. The more the saints prayed the better he felt. When prayer stopped the pain increased. He could recognize people he knew in his visions who were praying for him. The pain seemed to intensify during the Saturday afternoon baseball game—very few people's minds seemed to be concentrated on prayer for Bob just then!

On Sunday morning Bob was suffering acutely with pain. Everything from his waist down had stopped working. It was still hell for him at 10:04 A.M. when all his friends were gathered in church. At 10:05 Bob suddenly felt normal. It just seemed as though he had never been ill! He got up immediately and went around to the Baptist church to testify to their answered prayer and the healing power of God.

New Fellowship Promised

The word of the Lord came to Bob again: "I am raising up a group of young people in the south of Kansas City. They will not reject you, nor will they turn away from me!"

This left Bob searching the city and crying out to God, "Will they ever come, Lord?"

And the Lord appeared to him again. "They will be there by the spring of 1983 and these will be the signs: Before the snows are melted on the first day of spring they will accept you. They will be in the south of the city. They will speak about intercession and revival and they will be led by a twenty-seven-year-old man."

Since Bob and Viola needed Christian fellowship they had to join another church in the meantime. Bob explained to the minister from the beginning that they were only there temporarily and told him about the prophecy and that they would be leaving in the spring of 1983.

Checking out Bob's Story

All this was corroborated for Mike Bickle later. After he had known Bob a couple of weeks Mike felt he ought to go and seek the minister of that church to check out the strange prophet.

"Do you know a brother called Bob Jones?" asked Mike.

"Of course," replied the minister. "He was a member of our church for three years."

"Do you think he is a prophet?"

"Oh, yeah! He sure is. I've never known anything like his gift in my life."

"What kind of a guy is he?"

"He's a tremendous friend of mine."

"How do you feel about his leaving you?"

"Oh, I'm quite at peace about that because he told us openly from the beginning—when he first came to us three years ago—that as soon as 'the young people' arrived he would have to go off and join them. I'm right behind him because I am sure he is doing the will of God."

Mike Bickle was still ignorant of much of Bob Jones's background and he had to admit that he felt very wary about it all. He would have been wary anyhow but he felt that since he had had a personal word of warning from the Lord about a false prophet he had to be extra careful.

Now that Bob and Viola were worshipping regularly and happily at Kansas City Fellowship it was understandable that Mike should continue to keep a rather watchful eye on Bob.

CALLING THE CITY TO PRAYER AND FASTING

I t was March 1983. Art Katz was in town. Piloted by a friend, he had flown into Kansas City in a private plane. Art was the author of a best-selling book called *Ben Israel* where he tells his own story of being a Jew in search of meaning to life, which he finds eventually through faith in Jesus Christ. Art and Mike were old friends and they had been catching up with each other's news on Saturday. Art intended to fly out early on Sunday. Sunday came but the weather was unsuitable for flying.

Art planned to make the best of the unavoidable delay. He would now be able to visit the Kansas City Fellowship. It would be an opportunity to worship with them and talk to some of the congregation.

Prophet Greets Special Visitor

It was after the morning worship when Mike was engaged in praying for the sick that he just happened to glance across the church. There, to his great consternation, he saw Bob Jones ambling towards Art Katz, who was sitting at the back. Mike gasped inwardly. He had not mentioned anything about Bob

Jones to his friend. And there was no way to warn him now. Whatever would Art think about the members of the new congregation he was meeting? He clearly would not be leaving Kansas City with quite the impressions that Mike would have liked him to have! "It's no use," thought Mike, "I'll just have to trust the Lord to sort it all out."

By then Bob was already talking earnestly to Art. "He is probably used to handling nuts in any case!" thought Mike. "He will soon nail Bob as a false prophet. In fact, this could all turn out to be a real help—having Art's wisdom on the subject." Mike calmed himself with such reasoning and returned to his praying. A little later he glanced up again only to see they were still talking together! "Whatever is going on?" he wondered. When Bob had finished, Art came over to Mike looking disturbed and asked rather intently, "Who was that guy?"

"I don't think I really know," Mike replied. Adopting a role of ignorance and intentional nonchalance he was plainly dissociating himself from any responsibility for the embarrassing report he thought he was about to hear.

The Secrets of My Life

"That man is a prophet of God!" said Katz. "He told me secrets of my heart which no man could possibly know!"

Mike suppressed a cry as if in pain. He just could not allow himself to be taken for a ride by a false prophet—wherever and whoever he might be. It was a long day for Mike as he continued to ponder the problem of Bob Jones over and over in his mind.

That same evening Art approached Mike looking extremely distressed. "Mike, I'm burning up! I feel such an urgency to see that man once more. I have to talk to him. I know it's late [it was 9:00 P.M.] but is there any way I can see him again?"

"I'll call him up and see." Mike dialed and waited till Bob picked up the phone. "Hi! This is Mike. Bob, you know that guy from the church you spoke to this morning . . ."

"Yeah! I know him," said Bob, adding, "I've been waiting for you to call me all day!"

Mike silently gulped but keeping his voice low-key, he said, "Hey! How would you like to meet with us right now?"

"I'd love that," said Bob.

"Right!" said Mike. "We'll be over right away. It'll be me, Diane, Art, his pilot, Bob Scott, and a few others—six or seven!"

When they arrived they all sat around talking and Bob began to tell Art some more things about himself. Suddenly Art stood up and pronounced, "I don't care what kind of reproach you may receive, Bob. I will stand up and bear your rejection with you because you are a prophet of God!"

A Private and Personal Sign

As Mike was telling this story to the church, he shared with them in an aside something he said he had never told anyone before.

"This is such a dynamic thing! This centers around my brother Pat, who broke his neck playing high school football in 1973. Many of you probably read about that in the newspapers at the time. It was all over the front pages and on the radio. I was then studying at Washington University. I quit soon after because I wanted to be committed to the Christian ministry.

"My father came up to visit me at the university and we had a very serious talk. He said, 'Mike, we have a problem. I won't be around forever and your five sisters can't take on Pat. I know you love the Lord. I want you to make a covenant with

82

me for all the days of your life. Will you vow before the Lord that you will take the responsibility for looking after Pat?' ''

Mike did not hesitate for a moment.

'' 'Dad, I promise I'll do that,' I said, 'it will be an easy thing,' and as I said that a phrase from one of the latest hit songs flashed into my mind: 'He's not heavy; he's my brother and I love him so much!' I took that as a very precious word from the Lord to me and I have often turned it back to him in my prayers for my brother! 'Yes, Dad, I promise I will do that!' I reassured my father.

"I had never told anyone about that special prayer—not even my brother or my wife—it was just such a powerful, personal thing for me. Before we got married when I was courting Diane I explained to her simply about my commitment to Pat so she would know what she was taking on.''

He says he had never mentioned that special prayer to anyone because to someone else it could easily sound stupid.

Around Midnight

As they were still seated with Art Katz around Bob Jones's table that Sunday evening talking, praying, and weeping before the Lord, midnight came.

Suddenly Bob said to Mike, "By the way, I saw you in a vision last night, and I made a comment to you about the heavy responsibility you bore concerning Pat. You replied: 'He's not heavy; he's my brother and I love him so much.' ''

Mike was visibly startled at those words and began to sob. "You can have no idea what you have just said to me! Those were the very words that I had used in my secret covenant with the Lord over my brother!" he sobbed. "Not one single person ever knew that! You must, indeed, have been sent from God!"

Dazed, Mike was pondering to himself, "How would this day have ended if Art Katz had left early this morning as he had planned? None of us would ever have been here. God has certainly ordained this!"

What Day Is it Today?

Bob Jones startled Mike out of his distraction by asking, "What day is it today?" Though Mike was lost in his thoughts and did not catch the question addressed to him there was an answer.

"I don't know. It's Sunday!" someone murmured.

"Think! What day is it today?" Bob pressed the question with unusual insistence.

"It's March 21," said Mike, getting back on to Bob's wavelength at last.

"Yes, it's the first day of spring!" said Bob. "Why didn't Art Katz leave today?" He was pressing again for an answer.

"It was because of the snowstorm," replied Mike.

"Look outside!" said Bob. "What's happening?"

"The snows are melting!" they chorused.

"Thus saith the Lord!" said Bob, who now and then would fall back on the odd phrase from his favorite King James Version of the Bible. "On the first day of spring, before the snows melt, you will accept me around the table. This night has been ordained of the Lord. Truly you must hear the word that I bring to you, for God wants you to believe these things." They were certainly all "believers" now.

They went on through the night worshipping and weeping before the Lord.

Bob said, "There's a sovereign movement of God being birthed which will reach to the ends of the earth; the Lord gave me that very secret between himself and Mike, which no man could have known, to verify his prophecy."

Finally Mike rose from his seat at last and embraced Bob, saying, "Truly you are a prophet of the Lord!"

That was March 21, 1983.

Comet Surprise for Scientists Predicted

Then Bob reminded Mike what he had already prophesied across the city—that there would be a comet whose coming was totally unpredicted by scientists. This would come as a sign of God from the heavens of his promised moving upon Kansas City. Mike was left amazed and wondering, "Would God deign to give such a sign—a comet—as confirmation of this promise?"

Not everyone in Kansas City and the nation was happy about Bob's sudden recognition as a prophet of the Lord nor the leadership's preoccupation with his strange prophecies. There was a tremendous amount of rejection.

But then they could hardly have appreciated the sovereign way that God had brought Bob Jones across Mike's path and how Mike finally had been convinced. And because of Mike's own uncertainties about Bob Jones's prophetic authenticity he had not known what exactly to share with the congregation and when to do this. Besides, Mike had yet to learn how to blend the ministry of a prophet with his own public ministry of preaching, teaching, and leadership. Public church gatherings were not usually the best places for communicating this kind of prophecy—often given in enigmas and parables. Such revelations needed weighing sensitively, interpreting wisely, and applying appropriately.

Mike was still learning and had much to discover the hard way. This experience, combined with the wisdom he has gathered through the study of God's Word, makes what he has to teach on this subject today tremendously helpful. Some of his valuable insights will be elaborated upon in chapter 10.

Call the Solemn Assembly

Now it was April 1983. The fellowship had been meeting to pray every single night for five or six months. It was a Wednesday night, April 13, when the Lord spoke again directly to Mike Bickle. It was that internal audible voice again.

God said, "Call the people together for a solemn assembly. Call the people together to fast and pray for twenty-one days! This people in the heart of the nation will be like Daniel who, when the children of Israel were in captivity in Babylon, went on a twenty-one-day fast" (Dan. 10:2–3).

Mike Bickle understood that this was the key to the release of the children of Israel.

The words continued: "There will be five hundred people in this city. They will stand before God as Daniel did because there are promises for this nation as there were for the children of Israel. This nation is in bondage just like the children of Israel. And God wants to free this nation just as he did the children of Israel."

He said, "I am going to raise up a Daniel from the heart of this nation as I did from the children of Israel. Read on from Daniel, chapter 9! Five hundred people will come together and they will fast for twenty-one days and they will seek my face and that will be the beginning of my purposes in a new dimension for this nation!"

Mike was trembling—scared to death! However could he get up and say that? He was only a very young and new minister in town. He could imagine the charges of presumptuousness which would be leveled against him if he ever dared to do such a thing through a citywide summons.

He told his wife Diane and shared his fears with her. "Darling," he said, "God has just told me to call a solemn assembly from this city to fast and pray." The Kansas City Fellowship was having regular Sunday meetings for three hundred to four hundred people by then, and God had said there would be five hundred who would respond to this call. Mike finished by repeating what God had told him: "You lift up your voice and I will move the people! Do it because you have no choice. This is a command!"

Diane was dumbfounded. She found it hard to make any suggestions that would help him. "All I know," she said, jokingly, "is that if things go wrong I'm sure we can go back to St. Louis!"

Mike was surprised to sense in his spirit that he was becoming a little more resolved on the matter. "I'm going to give it a shot," he murmured, as if to test his own reaction. "If we are done in this city we are done, but I know I've got to do it if this is really God. I'll call Bob Jones in the morning."

It was April 14. He called Bob. "Bob, I have not known you for long but I know you are a prophet of the Lord. I have had a very scary word from the Lord that you don't know about."

"Yeah, I already know about it!" came Bob's calm, drawling reply.

"Amazed" was hardly the word for it—this was all just too bizarre for words to Mike!

Bob said he had already "seen" it and pressed Mike to come over right away.

Mike grabbed a couple of witnesses to take with him and they jumped into his car.

An Enigmatic Dialogue

When they reached Bob's home he came out to greet them all and then sat them down as Mike launched into what was on his mind.

"Bob, I really need a word from the Lord right now!"

Bob replied, "I have the word from the Lord already."

"What do you have?" asked Mike.

"I saw him," said Bob.

"Who did you see?"

He said, "You know who I saw!"

Mike replied, "Bob, I did not see anyone. That's not how God spoke to me! Who did you see?"

He was feeling a little peeved and impatient with this cat-and-mouse approach. Each of them believed he had had a revelation from God but was using the other's revelation to confirm his own. It seemed important for each not to give too much away while hoping that the other would corroborate it through the recounting of his own revelation. Hence this frustrating, enigmatic, step-by-step kind of dialogue.

Bob said, "I saw the Angel Gabriel."

"What did the Angel Gabriel say?"

"He said: 'Give the young man Daniel, chapter 9, and he will understand!' "

"That's incredible," thought Mike to himself. "We really have got to do this thing after all—we've really got to summon a twenty-one-day fast."

Aloud he inquired, "Will anyone respond to the call?"

And Bob replied, "He said there would be five hundred people!"

The same number exactly that the Lord had said to Mike—five hundred! It was truly the word of the Lord!

So Mike made a citywide call for a solemn fast to begin on May 7. Just as he had feared, there was opposition: the pastor of a leading church in town condemned the unknown upstart for his audacity. Mike found that kind of attack particularly difficult. Criticism from the world was predictable. Condemnation from leading men of God was totally unexpected. A gentle scolding in private from an older, more experienced Christian, maybe. But not condemnation from a church leader!

88

Tense Time in the Spirit

The next days were spent tensely waiting. Then the days of prayer and fasting began. The first night more than seven hundred crowded in to the church. They knew that, because the building seated seven hundred people and many were standing. They could hardly believe it! The next morning there was even more unbelievable news. Bob Jones brought the papers to Mike and pointed to the headlines. A comet unpredicted by scientists was coming across the nation, just as the Lord had said.

Mike gasped, "The Angel Gabriel and a comet! Incredible! I can't handle this, it's too much."

I asked Mike for details of that fasting and prayer and he told me that they prayed through nonstop from 6:00 A.M. to 12:00 midnight. One person after another would simply come to the microphone and begin to pray. They found themselves praying for many things over and over again.

Reporting later on those three weeks of fasting and prayer, when the average attendances were two hundred daily and five hundred nightly, Mike commented, "That was probably one of the most horrible times of my life, to be honest. We felt so weak and barren." But he realized that that was exactly what the Lord was trying to teach them. God had spoken to them from 1 Corinthians 15:42,43: "The body is sown in corruption, it is raised in incorruption. It is sown in dishonor, it is raised in glory. It is sown in weakness, it is raised in power."

Three Months of Drought Promised

On the last day of the fast Bob Jones got up and proclaimed a message to the city and the state.

"As the ark of the Lord was hidden in Obed Edom's house for three months and as Moses was hidden for three months in the cradle, so also there will be the total withholding of everything for three months, although God will allow a little bit of liberty.

"In this city everything will be withheld. For three months there will be a drought. That's the sign! God has spoken! The drought for three months is because the people have rejected the call to fast—they have mocked God. There will be rain on August 23."

Bob had given a specific date for rain during the drought which he predicted was about to begin.

This level of prophecy could certainly be scary! Mike found himself becoming an expert weather watcher. The weather, of course, was soon a matter of widespread public concern. To quote Mike:

"Kansas City was one of the bread-baskets of the world; it was the center of grain farming, fanning out to a radius of five hundred miles.

"The drought did not begin immediately. In fact there was heavy rain in June, but for the whole of July it was dry. It was terrible.

"No rain still during the first week of August or the second or the third. It was terrible! Bob Jones said the Lord had told him rain would come on August 23. We had all been poised since early dawn that day but by 1:00 P.M. there was still no rain. By six o'clock we were just resigned to wait for another day when suddenly it began. And did it rain? It poured! No man could have manipulated that. It just had to be God!"

That was still not the end of the drought, however. Although it was not a total withholding of rain, the exceedingly dry period covered a full three months, except for the predicted break on August 23. Official records reveal that it was the second lowest recorded rainfall for that period of time in the history of Kansas City!

Three More Years of Humiliation Predicted

For three months God had humiliated the city because it had mocked and ridiculed. But now for three years, God told them through Bob Jones, he was going to humiliate the Kansas City Fellowship. God always resists the proud. He had to teach these people he was choosing to use that his strength could only be made perfect in their weakness.

CHAPTER EIGHT

PROMISE OF REVIVAL

After the three weeks of fasting and prayer, soon followed by the three months of drought, the church braced itself for the three years of humiliation. God would reveal to them their utter weakness before he began to release his blessing through them according to his promises.

The incredible signs God had so sovereignly bestowed upon the leadership would serve as a wonderful preparation for any sacrifice which he might require from them. Now they tried to settle down patiently, resolving not to waver. Nevertheless they viewed the three long years ahead with a sense of awe and of their total unworthiness.

August 23 found them all giving glory to God for the coming of the rain on the day Bob Jones had predicted. There was still a month of drought to go. However, it was not long after it had ended that they were having to reassure each other that there really had been a drought. By mid-October they were doubting that it had happened after all.

November began with some people asking, "Who was that Bob Jones, anyway?" By this time Mike Bickle had developed a serious throat condition. Surgery had been recommended, but

Mike was still waiting on God over it. The church was getting difficult. People were grumbling and unhappy.

Yet One More Sign

On November 7 Bob Jones appeared at the door of Mike's office announcing that he had another "word"!

"The Lord says that you are an unbelieving people."

Mike, relating this later, said that he had thought of himself up to that moment as a very believing person!

"He says that he will give you yet one more sign!"

Mike sat back with a smile.

"I love this. What is it?"

So Bob continued: "The Lord says that on November 15 the word of the Lord will come to you in such a way that you will not waver in unbelief again. He says that he wants his people to believe so that his people are willing to make sacrifices for him."

Mike: "What's it going to be?"

Bob: "It will be straight from heaven!"

Mike, somewhat cynically: "That sounds exciting! I have not had too many of that kind of experience! It would seem that either I have to go up to heaven or someone has to come down if it's to be straight from heaven!"

Bob: "Sounds something like that to me too, though you never know with these prophecies!"

An Appointment with God

November 15 arrived—the big day! Mike was waiting, not really knowing how to approach such a prediction. Never before had he had to await a divine ministration of this kind. He tried praying, "Here I am Lord," and so on, though he felt the Lord would know that anyhow! He found it difficult to stay sitting for more than twenty minutes or so. He frequently got up to serve himself a cola or something of the sort. He lasted as long as he could and then gave up. It had not worked!

It was nighttime and he happened to spot a book by Howard Pittman, a Baptist preacher. Someone from across the city had sent it to him in the mail, but he had not had time to read it. Mike casually glanced at it and was quickly captivated by the story.

Pittman had been a policeman for thirty-five years and after retirement had opened an orphanage. In August 1979 he had had a death experience in the local hospital intensive care unit that lasted from the Friday to the following Monday. During that time his spirit left his body and he found himself standing before the Lord. Pittman heard himself saying, "Lord, I have been faithful to you all my days and I want my life back again. I have orphans in my care. I have faithfully preached the gospel. I regularly gave out tracts," and he reminded the Lord also of many other good things he had done.

Weekend in Eternity

Howard Pittman stood before the Lord in his spirit for those four days, intermittently passing in and out of death in that intensive care unit. Suddenly he heard the Lord addressing him: "Your life is an abomination in my sight!" In his mind Howard Pittman was saying, "Lord, that can't be true." But each time he protested, the word of the Lord came thundering back to him with awesome wrath: "Your life is an abomination." Six times he heard the Lord repeating those terrible words until he finally knelt down before him and said, "Holy Lord, forgive me. I've been a proud and arrogant man. I've done all these good works in my own name.'' The Lord replied, ''That's true! I will forgive you and I love you very much. I ordain you, my son, to take a word to my people for these days.'' He gave him a five-point message.

The Church that Made God Sick

Two of these points seemed especially relevant to Mike Bickle that night. One was that he was to tell the people that this was the Laodicean age and he would spit the Church out of his mouth because it was neither hot nor cold. He could find hardly a pure thing in the Church today—so much of it would have to change radically! The Lord explained to Howard that the reason he had wounded him was that his brothers would try to steal this message from his heart. ''You must know,'' said the Lord, ''that it is I who am speaking to you and that is why I allowed you to experience my wrath.''

The other point was that Howard was commissioned to go and tell God's people that signs and wonders would begin occurring increasingly, and they would be greater than anything the early apostles ever witnessed. Howard had a strong theological objection to signs and wonders and protested. The Lord said: ''You are greatly mistaken, for I will manifest my glory on the earth. Go down now for an appointed time and teach my people these things. Mark the date, for on this day I am going to begin to enlist my soldiers for the Lord's army.'' (This sounded very much like ''Joel's army'' which Paul Cain had talked about.) ''I want you to mark the date,'' he continued. ''On this very day I am going to begin the slow process of vomiting my church from my mouth.''

The Lord said: ''Go and tell the brethren to be patient, for though it will begin in my heart there will yet be a season of waiting and they must not grow weary, because it is I the Lord who am doing this."

That Was It!

As Mike Bickle was reading, he thought, "It all sounds just like us here." He began checking the dates. Howard Pittman's death experience was in August 1979. The "solemn assembly" for prayer and fasting in Kansas City began on May 7, 1983. The comet came on May 7, 1983. He double-checked the date the Lord had told Howard Pittman to mark—the day was May 7, 1983! Mike looked up. "Oh, my God! This is the revelation!" All the time he had been thinking that he must have missed it.

He looked up to heaven: "Lord, how could this be? It's amazing! You sent Howard Pittman on ahead of time so that his testimony could be a confirmation of your other prophecies to me when I came to read his book on this day—November 15!"

That was the sign from heaven for the whole church which the Lord had told Bob Jones Mike would receive on November 15 so that he, the leader of the Kansas City Fellowship, might never again doubt God.

"My purposes are established," the Lord declared plainly to Mike (whether in a vision or simply to his thoughts, he does not say), and went on, "I am moving on the earth. This commenced on May 7, 1983. Tell the nations of the earth!"

Mike was shaking his head in awesome wonder. "God! Why do you want these people so much to believe this?"

"So that they might be patient and understand the gravity of it," came the solemn reply.

Those three years of waiting ended in May 1986. In June Mike's serious and chronic throat condition became remarkably improved!

Angels Overheard

Way back in the mid-1970s Bob Jones had a vision, which has already been referred to, where he overheard a conversation between two angels.

One said, "You know the Lord is about to begin one of his mighty works in the midst of this city."

The other replied, "Oh! Is that so? When is the Lord about to begin and where?"

He heard the first angel say: "He's going to begin a mighty work in the midst of this city which will move to the ends of the earth. As this part of America is one of the bread-baskets of the world in the natural, so also it shall become the bread-basket of the world in the spiritual."

The second angel asked, "How do you know?"

And the first replied, "There are a number of signs."

(Bob felt these signs were in some strange way parables. They are significant for the story now.)

"1. There would be 50,000 people gathered in the Lord's name as one sign.

"2. There would be a further gathering of 500,000 as another sign.

"3. Another sign would be the eruption of Mount St. Helens on the northwest coast of the United States.

"4. Another sign would be worldwide famine.

"5. The Lord would raise up faithful and mature intercessors from Kansas City.

"6. Teams would go out from Kansas City to many places."

(Mike Bickle is always careful to stress how the Lord has shown them that theirs is not by any means the only center which God was committing himself to use in this way. And there was going to be a lot of cross-pollination between the centers. There could be no room for pride. One of the marks of the Lord's army would be that its soldiers were humble. There were many streams which flowed into the river, which made glad the city of God—and the KCF was just one of them!)

"7. A great explosion of light would go out from this city." (Bob was shown a flash of brilliant white light exploding in the heart of Kansas City and out to the nation and it was impressed upon him that this would be the sign for the fulfillment of this prophecy.) "The movement will have global significance like the flash of an atomic blast which occurs even though multitudes may not see it."

No One Believed Him

Bob Jones began to share these visions with others; this was before the Kansas City Fellowship had arrived in town. No one could understand what he was talking about, and since he had not fully comprehended them himself this was not surprising. "There will be 50,000 gathered in Kansas City, then 500,000 in Washington," he boldly proclaimed. People thought he was mad. What Bob did not know was that there would be a time lag before this happened as is so often the case with prophecy. In fact some 50,000 gathered at a large charismatic conference in the Arrowhead Stadium—Truman's Sports Complex—at Kansas City in 1977. A similar celebration with 500,000 met in Washington three years later.

Most people had forgotten Bob's prophecy by then, but Bob himself was very excited when the 50,000 gathered in Kansas City, and he was most perplexed when the newspapers reported a crowd of only 350,000 at Washington!

He complained to the Lord about the lesser numbers, "What went wrong, Lord? I missed it!"

But the Lord answered, "Who do you believe, Bob, the newspapers or me?"

The other signs have been fulfilled: the eruption of Mount

St. Helens, the tragic famines, and the raising up of intercessors in Kansas City.

Mississippi Sign Confirms Promise of Coming Revival

In early 1983 Bob and Mike were chatting together when Bob referred again to his white horse vision. He explained that the white horse he had seen was in a stream of water about four inches deep. (The white horse always appeared to symbolize the corporate work of God in Bob's vision.) Bob had seen this stream turn into a flood and the Lord had told him that once there were 500 committed intercessors in the Kansas City Fellowship (by then meeting in their new Grandview Worship Center) there would be an explosion of membership into 5,000. They now had 1,500 people regularly attending worship, but there were not yet 500 actually committed to the ministry of intercession.

The prediction was that once they had the 500 the flood would come instantly and in one hour they would be 5,000. The prophet was shown that the majority of the added 4,500 would be leaders and lapsed Christians who had fallen away over the past twenty years or so. They would be those who had had a clear call in the 1960s, 1970s, and 1980s and had since lost it or fallen into sin and unbelief. God was going to show mercy on them. It was almost as if they had been prepared and were in waiting. The 4,500 would quickly be mobilized into new wineskins that would be capable of containing the new wine: the new converts. So the first outpouring would not be primarily to bring in new believers but to restore old ones who would constitute the leadership for the new wineskins. Mike remembered that when Bob passed all this on to him, he had added matter-of-factly, "The angel said: 'That's the strategy! The sign will be "Mississippi"!' "

In that vision the Lord had revealed that the numbers would

increase from 500 to 5,000 by multiplication; then 5,000 to 10,000 by addition; then 10,000 to 15,000 by addition; then 15,000 to 20,000 by addition; and then 20,000 to 25,000 by addition. (A strange way of saying the numbers were going to increase. It would have seemed simpler to say from 500 to 25,000!) Mike and Bob were intrigued by the sign "Mississippi." They looked it up in every book they thought could give them a relevant clue. Mississippi, Mississippi! Whatever could it mean?

Then one May day Bob Jones came into the prayer meeting waving the latest edition of the *Kansas City Star* with the headline MISSISSIPPI FLOOD KEEPS 10,000 FROM HOMES. This seemed to be part of the sign. The prophecy was beginning to make sense.

Noel is Coming!

One Tuesday night in 1984 Bob Jones suddenly announced at the prayer meeting that Noel was coming! No one had any idea what it meant and the leadership pressed him for further details. But Bob said that that was all the Lord had told him to say. There were plenty of jokes going the rounds after that. Did it mean Christmas was coming? What else could it be?

On the following Friday Mike was at a pastors' gathering, where he was surprised to meet a South African named Noel who was a pastor working on the other side of the city. The two had never met before. Noel had a tremendous burden for intercession and revival which matched Mike's exactly, and so it was quite natural for them to want to meet again. They did so that night after the KCF time of intercession, which ended at 10:00 P.M. Mike took along one or two other friends and they shared their common interest in prayer and revival, talking well into the night. Mike was so fascinated that he suggested, to Noel's surprise, that they meet yet again the next day and Noel agreed.

Mike was wondering if God might be calling Noel to join

them in leadership for the KCF but he needed to be especially cautious in view of the Lord's personal warning to him. There would have to be some very clear indications from the Lord. Was this the Noel of that enigmatic pronouncement earlier in the week when Bob had said, "Noel is coming"?

Major-General Alexander

The next morning Noel shared with Mike a remarkable vision he had had from the Lord which was very precious to him and seemed to fit in with what Mike had been talking about. He was in Colorado. He felt the Lord calling him to spend time with him in prayer. It was way into the night. Then the Lord told him to stand up and look to the north. He asked Noel what he saw.

"I told him I saw a valley full of thousands and thousands of lilies."

"He said, 'They will be your inheritance. Those blooms represent the souls you will bring to me. Now look to the south. What do you see?' "

Noel looked at another valley stretching away in the distance and again it was just full of thousands and thousands of lilies.

"These are the souls you will also bring to me!"

When Noel heard that he just wept and wept.

As Mike was listening to this he marveled and praised God. He said, "I must take you to meet Bob Jones right now. I'll call him. I can almost guarantee that he already knows we are coming."

He called Bob on the phone. "Hello Bob! I have got a man here . . ."

"Yeah! I know. Bring him over."

Mike was not even surprised any more. They were soon at Bob's house.

"Yeah! You're the one," muttered Bob as they entered. "What's your name?"

"Noel Alexander," said the South African.

Bob was rummaging through his rather grubby pile of papers— a collection of some twenty-five of the thousands of visions he had had from the Lord that he had specially written down. These were the ones which were still puzzling him.

"Here we are!" he said. "Vision of November 1976: When Major-General Alexander is released then it will be a new step in God's purpose for this move!"

Bob had kept the vision from 1976 to that date in 1984. He now addressed Noel: "God wants me to put a mirror in front of you. When I tell you something you will see your life and when you see your life you will know that God wants you to understand something more that I will show you.

"The Lord showed you to me as a man who stood before a valley of many, many flowers—he showed you multitudes of flowers and he has told you that this represented your inheritance as part of his body."

Though God had only told this to Noel recently, he had revealed to Bob, as far back as 1976, that "Major-General" Alexander would be used to bring thousands and thousands into the kingdom of God. Bob said he had never been able to figure out the "Major-General" bit. He had a friend at the Pentagon whom he had asked to identify this Major-General Alexander for him, but according to his friend there was no general in the U.S. Army by that name. Perplexed, Bob had stored the vision away for its proper time.

Meeting with Paul Cain Predicted

On one occasion after they had come to know each other well Bob came to Mike and asked him, "Are you picking anything up from the Lord?"

"No," said Mike, "not that I am aware of."

"Well," replied Bob, "am I in sin? Can you see anything about me? Am I quenching the Holy Spirit?"

"No! Really, Bob, I am not aware of anything. Why?"

"Because the Lord has shut the whole thing down!"

"Whatever do you mean, Bob?"

"Well, I haven't seen a vision in two nights!"

Bob was used to seeing visions very frequently.

Before the end of the year, however, Bob Jones was getting a number of particular revelations about another older prophet somewhere whom the Lord was going to bring across his path, and though Bob was not given his name the man became clearly identifiable as Paul Cain. They had never met. Mike was intrigued.

In September the same year Mike was giving a ride to Agustine, traveling from Arizona to a conference in California organized by the Vineyard Ministries International (where incidentally I later realized I had first met Mike myself). On the way Agustine mentioned that he knew of a prophet called Paul Cain who received very significant revelations from God. Of course Mike was fascinated to learn all he could about him in view of his beneficial experience with prophets by that time.

They happened to stop along the way at a McDonald's where Mike caught sight of a face he recognized.

"Hi," said Mike, "what are you doing these days?"

"Oh!" replied the man, Reid Grafke by name, "I've been working with Paul Cain from Dallas since 1979."

Mike found the coincidence quite extraordinary and felt God alerting him that one day he was going to meet Paul face to face! He accepted, however, that God himself would arrange such a meeting his own way should that truly be his will. Mike was learning not to get ahead of God.

CHAPTER NINE

OUR INTERVIEW WITH THE PROPHETS

Whatever were we visitors to make of all these visions and signs? Some had clearly been fulfilled in most remarkable ways and others predicting revival *en masse* still awaited fulfillment. It was fascinating, coming from our rather cynical culture, to meet so many people who seemed to accept so easily the whole dimension of revelation at this level. We could almost understand why they believed it, but for us outsiders, who had not been involved in the gradual, step-by-step process of a movement of God through revelation and the subsequent fulfillment of signs, the novelty was mind-boggling.

On Sunday afternoon Mike Bickle had arranged for us to meet a number of the prophets in one of the church offices. I do not remember all those present, but besides Mike Bickle and Bob Jones I recall Jim Goll, John Paul Jackson, Mike Sullivant, and David Parker. There were also others who were on the staff. We were grateful for this opportunity to meet in a relaxed way and the abiding impression of that meeting was the openness to God, the readiness to listen, the deference each gave to the others, and their submission to Mike's authority as leader.

We inquired how they had all come together. It was a matter

of amazement to us that there could be so many prophets receiving such a high level of revelation from God who were all living in the same city and were all committed to the Kansas City Fellowship. Most of them had found themselves rejected in their previous churches. Truly, as Jesus said of himself, a prophet has no honor in his own country (Matt. 13:57). It appeared that this coming together had been brought about through the Lord's direct overruling. Unbeknown to each other they had prayed, and the Lord had told them that Kansas City was to be a prophetic city and that they had been drawn there by the spirit of God like moths at night to a lighted candle. God had told them to get up and move to the land of the anointing and "I will greatly bless you."

None of them had been aware of a secular history of Kansas City written about the year 1930 and handed down to David Parker. Its subtitle was "Kansas City—The Prophetic City"! David had only recently noticed this and had communicated it to Mike and the rest of the KCF staff.

Humanly speaking, had it not been for the wise, gracious, and thoroughly Bible-based leadership of Mike Bickle, they might well have had their prophetic gifting stifled to death. This, it now seems probable, is most commonly the case in the Christian Church.

There were several things, obviously, that we were wanting to ask these prophets, and perhaps the fact that there were four of us to ask such questions and so many of them to answer meant that we did not find out all we wanted to know. Perhaps we never will!

How are Prophecies Received?

Our first question was: How do prophets receive their revelations. Is it through the "psyche" (soul) or the "pneuma" (spirit)?

105

This was important for us to clarify. For the average Christian the word "psychic" is tainted by its association with the occult, but in fact the Greek word "psyche" is a wholesome New Testament word translated "soul." Such a good biblical word clearly needs redeeming today. The psychic center in each of us seems to have a vital role to play in the area of revelation from God.

Then if occultists get limited communication from the powers of darkness on to the psyche, which some claim to be the case (though obviously such revelations, even when true, have an evil origin for evil objectives), then such a counterfeit must be matched by a genuine experience from God almighty. Wherever there is the counterfeit there must be the genuine reality. No one would be deceived by a $13 bill. It must clearly be false because there are no genuine $13 bills in circulation. But anyone might be deceived by a counterfeit $10 bill.

The consensus among the prophets in answer to our question seemed to be that the psyche was involved in their visions. They were clearly neither embarrassed nor threatened in any way by our description of their gifts as psychic in the pure sense. Of course, this is an area where it is impossible to be anything but tentative because there has not yet been found any scientific way of distinguishing between soul and spirit. We cannot take a soul and preserve it in a test tube or take a spirit and dissect it under a microscope. And who among those who might object to Christians using the term can prove in fact that occultists themselves really do operate through the psyche? Or who will argue that because spiritualists profess to operate through the spirit world we Christians must avoid the use of the word spirit in our religious experience or theology?

Insofar as these prophets seemed to have had a large number of revelations that have proved in time to be true, have served the common good and have been glorifying to God, their views were worth hearing. They seemed to have no problem in accepting the term psychic in this pure sense to describe one part of the process of divine revelation to human beings.

The human spirit is a channel that picks up spiritual transmissions from God or from the powers of darkness, and these are reflected on to the screen of the psyche, the soul. The same TV channel can carry beastly cruelty, pornography, or breathtaking beauty. The responsibility for the subject matter lies not in the channel itself but in the source of the transmission or the choice of the person tuning into the program.

The antennae of the spirit appear to involve, among other things, possibly, the counterparts of the physical senses. The psalmist hinted at something of the kind when he said, "Taste and see that the Lord is good." The transmissions are tasted, smelled, seen, heard, and felt. For these prophets all the senses might be spiritually operative when they receive communication from God but probably most of them would use initially one "sense." They stressed the need of training in this through constant use (Heb. 5:14). At the end of our session, when these brethren were about to prophesy over us, Bob Jones turned to John Paul Jackson and said: "You had better start, brother—I can see the anointing on your eyes." It was a strange expression to our ears, but even stranger, I had already seen the anointing on him with my own eyes.

To some God vouchsafed open visions where the picture or the word was very clear and at other times enigmatic speech, riddles, and parables.

How to be Receptive Channels

"Is there anything we need to avoid that might obstruct reception?" we asked. It was clear these men all had a supreme commitment to "follow after holiness" and their comments would be most helpful.

John Paul shared how the Lord had dealt with him over a problem he had had with occasionally confused visions that came to him as flashbacks resulting from watching TV too much. He said that for the prophetic ministry that God had given him, the more television he watched the fewer true visions from God he could experience.

Bob Jones agreed that the Lord would not let him watch much TV either. "I can't get into that fantasy realm—it cuts off my visions!"

They advised watching carefully against counterfeit visions of any kind. Someone mentioned alcohol as creating confusion, since when taken in excess people can begin to "see" things:

> The priest and the prophet . . . are swallowed up by wine . . . they err in vision, they stumble in judgment (Isa. 28:7).

Great care was needful indeed about anything which distracted the heart and the mind from God.

Another problem they shared was the danger of confusion over revelations where the person receiving them had particularly strong opinions, prejudices, or unresolved bitterness in certain areas. It was easy to distort such revelations and color their own interpretations. Such revelations should be jettisoned.

Anyone professing to have a revelation from God needs to ensure that his/her relationship with God is good. As the Lord said:

> "I have not spoken to them, yet they prophesied. But if they had stood in My counsel, and had caused My people to hear My words, then they would have turned them from their evil way" (Jer. 23:21–22).

Do Prophets Ever Get Things Wrong?

Mike Bickle was at pains to stress that he saw a real distinction between the recognized office of a prophet and those who received revelations and gave prophecies. At KCF they only actually regard Paul Cain as a prophet (he does not live in Kansas City and is not a member of Mike's staff), though the self-effacing Paul would never claim such an office for himself. This led on naturally to our next question. We asked tactfully if any of them was ever wrong.

They all agreed that they had occasionally been proved wrong. Sometimes their revelation was right but their interpretation or application was wrong. According to Mike Bickle, who confirmed that they certainly could be wrong, the problem seemed to be that they were right too often to be ignored. There was little problem over the revelations—the difficulties were more likely to be over the interpretations.

In the Old Testament they would have been put to death for giving false prophecy (Deut. 18:20); but Mike pointed to the grace of God who had instructed simply, through New Testament revelation, that their visions and prophecies should be weighed by others (1 Cor. 14:29).

No one should act on one prophecy alone. If it comes independently as a confirmation of something that God had already been speaking about in other ways, it certainly would be an encouragement to proceed in that direction. There is always the further check that if it is right there will be peace of heart about it (Col. 3:15). But if the revelation is something completely new and out of the blue, it is important to wait, watch, and pray for further confirmation.

We asked them how they felt about getting things wrong. They all agreed that it could be humiliating. Nowadays they have learned to offer their visions with some clear disclaimers to any idea of infallibility just in case anyone should want to assume a prophet could never err. But they still felt confused and sometimes rejected if they got it wrong. Sometimes, too, they thought they must be wrong and felt just as confused and rejected when they found out later that they had been right after all.

Bob Jones told of an occasion when he was at a meeting in his home church where there was a wonderful time of worship and praise, and the word of the Lord came to him: "Macaroni cheese"!

He naturally hesitated about speaking out such a word as that; it was just too stupid! But the word kept pressing on him and eventually he summoned the courage to speak it out. When he actually did call it out the congregation laughed so much he was really embarrassed. To make matters worse the pastor, who was obviously embarrassed as well, made light of it by suggesting that Bob must be hungry! At this point a whole family got up and walked out, which only intensified Bob's discomfort. He went home to his favorite place with God, his woodshed in the garden, and repented.

It was several months before he heard the other side of the story. An old saint of God, a widow who lived way out in the countryside, had a family of eleven. The eldest ten were all serving the Lord but she was very concerned about the youngest, a truck driver, still apparently godless. She told the Lord in her prayers that she was getting old and she wanted some assurance from the Lord about this wayward son before she died.

She had heard of Bob Jones and decided to visit the church where he normally worshipped. She asked the Lord to give her a sign which only she would understand. When she got there that crazy word from Bob Jones was just the assurance from God she needed. She was quite appalled when everyone laughed as she felt this was a sign of disrespect for God's prophet. She left with her family, both distressed and delighted—distressed for the church, delighted for herself. Her son drove a truck for a regular delivery service for macaroni cheese! She could not have had a better coded word of encouragement from the Lord!

Failure was something which most of them had felt very acutely at first but were learning to cope with better. This was partly due to the warm and understanding fellowship of the other prophets and partly to the very positive place being given to prophecy by the leadership. This meant that most of them now found they could cope much better with being shown to be wrong or even being misunderstood; but it was still painful.

Are Prophets Born with the Gift?

We wanted to know if they were all born with this gift. To our surprise we discovered that most of them now felt they had been called, like Jeremiah, from their mother's womb to their prophetic office. I have since talked to others with this gift only to find that often their offspring have had the gift also. (Such a discovery gives some insight into the comment of Amos, who claimed he was neither a prophet—not trained in any prophetic school, nor the son of a prophet—not born into a prophetic line (Amos 7:14). This could also explain why Paul seems to list prophecy as a natural talent (in Romans 12:6–8) yet still refers to it as a spiritual gift (in 1 Corinthians 12:10). This also helped us to see how those not born with the talent of prophecy could receive the gift of prophecy later in life.

David Parker seemed to be the only one among the prophets to whom the gift had come, or who discovered he had been given it, later in life. He had had an academic background and had at one time done some postgraduate studies at Regent's College in Vancouver. With faculty encouragement he had been tentatively feeling his way towards Cambridge to study for a Ph.D. when the Lord stopped him.

He had told David that he was a good student but he was looking for good disciples. This had changed the direction of David's life. David, who was brought up in Kansas City, has since founded and leads the Northside Fellowship Center (membership *c.* 250), which is one of the newer daughter churches of the KCF.

We then asked how anyone who desired this gift might receive it. They said that such a person would need to make a commitment to getting it and really wanting it (1 Cor. 14:1); to pray for it and to work with others who had it. It was also possible for someone who had the gift to impart it (Rom. 1:11; 1 Tim. 4:14; 2 Tim. 1:6); but Paul's injunction to "lay hands suddenly on no one" would also apply here. Where the gift had been ignored or unused for some time (as was probably the case with Timothy), it needed to be "stirred up" again.

It was a great help, they said, if one could get to be with others who already had such an anointing "as it kind of rubbed off on you"—it was like the mantle of Elijah falling on Elisha. Mantle prophets call forth other mantle prophets.

Finally, in using the gift some have just had to start "in proportion to . . . faith" with an impression (Rom. 12:6). No wonder Wimber spells faith R-I-S-K! The only real way to learn is through the experience of stepping out—like Peter who actually got out of the boat and walked a few paces on the water. When the Lord told Bob Jones to prophesy against abortion Bob asked the Lord how he was going to do that and the Lord told him to start doing it right there, where he was, in his truck. This proved to be a vital step in the development of his prophetic ministry.

David Parker tells how he was once lamenting that he, and others like him, did not have a spiritual father to teach him how to move into this supernatural ministry. He began to pray about this, and as he did so he saw himself in an old study with cobwebbed bookshelves, which he scanned for something suitable to help. At last his eye fell upon a musty old tome entitled, *The Ways of the Spirit,* which he took down eagerly only to find it was not really a book at all—it was a scrapbook.

On the first page was a tear-stained handkerchief; on the second, a blood-stained bandage from a child's knee, grazed from a fall; and so on. From this he understood that the Lord was showing him that one can learn these things only by experience.

Prophecy, it seems, may be a natural talent for those who have been born with it (Rom. 12:6–8), but always to be exercised properly in God's service it must be "in proportion to our faith." It is also seen in Scripture as a spiritual gift (1 Cor. 12:10), conveyed through the anointing of the Holy Spirit, and to be used for the common good. Finally, it seems that prophecy may also be imparted by another person who also has the same anointing (Rom. 1:11).

Are Prophecies Always Fulfilled?

"Do all the prophecies come to pass?" we asked.

"No," they said, "not all of them are meant to."

Usually negative prophecies pointing to death and destruction are given to indicate what the enemy is specifically intending to do, and these are to alert the saints to prayer. Jesus saw that Satan desired to sift Peter as wheat, which looked like it would be a terribly painful ordeal for him, but Jesus prayed for Peter to protect him.

But sometimes there can be no doubt that it is God's clear intention to bring immediate judgment upon a nation or to terminate the life of an individual. The Lord made this clear through Jeremiah when he said:

> The instant I speak concerning a nation and concerning a kingdom, to pluck up, to pull down, and to destroy it, if that nation against whom I have spoken turns from its evil, I will relent of the disaster that I thought to bring upon it. And the instant I speak concerning a nation and concerning a kingdom, to build and to plant it, if it does evil in My sight so that it does not obey My voice, then I

will relent concerning the good with which I said I would benefit it (Jer. 18:7–10).

The city of Nineveh was a case in point. The people repented and God withheld the promised judgment. That made Jonah angry. He felt that God's mercy on the Ninevites, once they repented, had undermined his own prophetic credibility. The Lord showed Amos that he was about to send a plague of locusts and a judgment of fire upon Israel. In each case Amos prayed the Lord not to let it happen and each time the Lord relented (Amos 7:3,6).

King Hezekiah was an example of God reconsidering a case in changed circumstances. God had warned Hezekiah through Isaiah (38:1) that he was to prepare to die but when Hezekiah prayed for a longer life, God gave him another fifteen years.

It is clear that the fulfillment of prophecy is not inevitable; usually it is conditional. Positive promises are often made clearly dependent upon one remaining faithful to God (Jer. 18:9–10), believing the promises and getting prepared for their fulfillment. Negative prophesying should be countered by repentance and prayer.

Is Prophecy Linked with Personal Holiness?

Is there a link between the prophet's character and this ability to prophesy? Was there a need to attain a certain level of holiness before one could be anointed with this gift? There are instances in the Bible where men had prophesied who were either corrupt like Balaam (Num. 24:17; Rev. 2:14); childish and angry like Jonah (Jon. 4:9); or hostile to Christ like Caiaphas (John 11:50; John 18:14). Our friends showed from the example of their own calls that God had anointed most of them in immaturity. The gift of prophecy was not contingent upon maturity or holiness but upon the sovereignty of God.

114

But they had no doubt that since major strands of their prophecy were concerned with justice and holiness—reflecting the character of God—he required a matching up with the prophets' own lives. As far as possible they should themselves be models of their prophecy and be seen to be worthy representatives of the author of the revelations. The fruit of their lips must equate with the fruit of their lives.

Jesus had said,

You will know them by their fruits. Do men gather grapes from thornbushes or figs from thistles? Even so, every good tree bears good fruit, but a bad tree bears bad fruit. A good tree cannot bear bad fruit, nor can a bad tree bear good fruit (Matt. 7:16–18).

LEADERSHIP VERSUS PROPHECY

B y this time I can imagine most church leaders beginning to wonder how they would ever cope with a prophet if one should show up in their congregation. It need not be difficult at all! Whenever I borrow someone else's car the first thing I want to know (assuming it is licensed, insured, and roadworthy) is how to drive the vehicle: "How do the gears operate and where are the brakes?" Once I know about these things, though I understand very little of the workings of the engine, I am ready to edge the vehicle onto the road. My approach would be much the same about raising a prophetic ministry in the local church. Once a leader recognizes the value of prophecy and understands how this ministry can be managed, even though he may understand very little of how it actually works, he is likely to be much more relaxed and to approach the subject more constructively.

The Dynamics Involved

It is helpful to sketch out some of the basic problems so that the pastor, the people, and the prophets can all understand the dynamics involved. It's probably a joke, because I never saw one on sale, but Mike says their tape called "Insecure Pastors and Rejected Prophets" was a best-seller! The title neatly says it all. There is the potential in any emerging prophetic ministry for major tensions. The person sharing a prophecy is naturally concerned about being received and obviously feels in need of positive encouragement when he is risking his own reputation.

The pastor knows that he has responsibility during any disorder and senses the need of the flock to be protected from ravening wolves or naive ego-trippers. The average congregation has a great accumulation of wisdom and is both concerned about being taken for a ride and offended that anyone should imagine they are going to allow themselves to be duped. They are also worried that their minister is unaware of how things could go wrong.

Further, especially if the person prophesying is a good person with the best of intentions, the question of authority is posed. If the prophecy comes directly from God, should the prophet take over the church? Does the one who speaks *ex dono* have a higher authority than the one who speaks *ex officio?* Does the eye no longer need the hand? That was the kind of confusing misunderstanding that brought about Edward Irving's downfall in his famous London Presbyterian church in the early 1830s. Out of his deep humility he mistakenly assumed that those with gifts of the spirit must in some way be superior to those with responsibility for government in the church.

Governmental Authority

But the duly appointed minister can never surrender the solemn responsibilities of his office; otherwise there will be spiritual anarchy. There was an occasion when the apostle Paul said, "I magnify my ministry" (Rom. 11:13). There may be occasions when a church pastor has to do the same.

In a recent article, Wayne Gruden points out significantly

that Peter never tells churches to be subject to prophets, but to *elders* (1 Pet. 5:5). Paul did not call the prophets of the Ephesian church to give them final counsel; he sent for the *elders* (Acts 20:17). Paul and Barnabas did not appoint prophets to govern every church; they appointed *elders* (Acts 14:23). Similarly Paul spoke of "the elders who rule well" (1 Tim. 5:17) and never of prophets ruling well. Peter told the *elders,* not the prophets, to "Shepherd the flock of God which is among you" (1 Pet. 5:2). The New Testament church is never seen to be governed by prophets or by prophecies.

No prophet has been given authority over the church; he does not have governmental authority. He may have authority—God's anointing—to prophesy, but if it is in the church then it must be under the authority of the leadership appointed by the church. The leadership may require him to desist from prophesying there at any moment and even forbid his prophesying altogether. Of course, the leader is accountable to God at all times for whatever course of action he may think it is right to take.

Not many prophets want to take over the leadership, but if they had real potential for church leadership they would not attempt to get it in that way. However, some leaders are prophets. We remember Moses who was both a prophet and one of the greatest human leaders in history, if not *the* greatest. Ezekiel was a priest besides being a prophet. And, of course, Jesus was a prophet, too—*the* prophet (Deut. 18:18 and John 4:14).

Some embryonic prophets unwittingly crave public visibility and have endeavored to get this from within a congregation for which they do not have responsibility and for whose upbuilding they have apparently done very little previously.

But should a leader ever feel a little insecure in the exercise of his office when confronted by a prophet who claims to have a message from the Lord (and there are often situations where a leader might easily feel threatened, especially where the situation

118

is new and he has no precedent for dealing with it), he should always remember that he has the proper authority to lead the church and the prophet does not. Indeed, his conduct in a leadership role would probably prove very inadequate, since that is not his particular gifting.

Too often the fact is that the pastor initially perceives the prophet as a threat to his leadership and, as such, one to be snuffed out speedily in the name of decency and order. In which case, should he wield the sword of authority too heavily, he may cut out the prophet's tongue completely and annihilate the possibility of a prophetic ministry altogether.

Jesus said that he who receives a prophet in the name of a prophet receives a prophet's reward (Matt. 10:41). Many church leaders have no idea how to receive a prophet and would be totally ignorant of both the role and function of prophecy in the church and the world today. They would not want their ignorance to be exposed either. But where can leaders possibly get positive help and enlightenment? How can such a ministry be fostered? How can nascent prophets be nurtured? They have no good models in their particular ecclesiastical tradition to help them to foster prophecy in the church so one of God's gifts for the church is stifled and dies. The church is much the poorer for it. And as someone has wittily put it: "If you don't have prophets you suffer losses!"

Limiting Prophecy

It is probably best at first to limit prophecy in church to the simple inspirational kind that we read about in 1 Corinthians 14:3 which is for edification, encouragement, and consolation. Other prophecy, such as the exposure of sin or exhortations about the church's future, should be brought to the leadership and left with them.

With regard to the latter kind of prophecy it is good initially for the person who believes he is receiving revelations from God to log a record of his prophecies privately. In this way he can double-check when his prophecy has been fulfilled and can be more assured that he is not being deceived or simply carried away on an ego trip. This at least will give him and the leadership the encouragement of some clear endorsement before it is expected that prophecies of that nature should in any way be shared with the church or acted on by the leadership. Too many want the prophet's notoriety before they have established a prophet's credibility. How could a church leader take such people seriously?

A little while ago I was talking to a lady in the north of England whom I happen to respect very much for her commitment to the Lord. She showed me a letter she was writing to one of our archbishops. In it she described how she had been in York Minster one day admiring the famous stained-glass rose window. As she did this the words "In three days I will destroy this temple" came vividly to her mind. She dismissed them thinking she was simply recalling relevant Scripture. But the words still kept leaping out at her. Suddenly she realized that it was not Scripture at all! What Jesus had actually said was: "Destroy this temple, and in three days I will raise it up" (John 2:19). She was greatly puzzled. Was it in fact a lot of rubbish? It so happened that in three days the Minster was struck by fire and the window and roof, among other things, had to be renovated.

I did not think it would help the archbishop very much to get such a letter, imagining some of the many an archbishop must receive! A completely negative response would not bring her much peace of heart, especially as she felt that having been shown something so significant it must have been for some purpose.

I told her I felt that the Lord could in fact be encouraging her with a prophetic ministry and that she should note down the occasions when she felt God was speaking to her and then record what happened as a result. In this way she would be able to establish a personal history of prophecy with which she could encourage herself to step out more boldly once it was quite plain that this was in fact a gift that God had given her. I think she began to feel this might be a constructive way in which to view the whole incident.

Someone who is attempting to keep a record like this can share it in a low-key, behind-the-scenes way with a leader who can then be a witness to any progress, which will be a help in the future to both. The aspiring "prophet" should also keep a record of the times when he has got it wrong, so that he can evaluate his gift and learn to see where he may have erred. If we cannot be absolutely honest with each other it is hard to see how leader and prophet can progress very far together.

This is the sort of approach that Mike Bickle has learned through hard experience and has developed in the KCF. He also makes a point of distinguishing between people who speak prophetically—those who prophesy and those who exercise the ministry of a prophet. He deals basically with both in the same way, though not all who prophesy become prophets (and he would be very slow to recognize such an office and even slower actually to call anyone a prophet); nevertheless, all prophets have to begin by prophesying.

He sees three distinct stages in the process of making prophecy edifying: the revelation itself; the interpretation of the revelation; and the application of the interpretation.

I. Revelation

I am not speaking here about how people actually receive revelations. We have seen some examples of that in the chapters on Paul Cain and Bob Jones. I am talking about the practical nature of revelations, the proper source for revelations and the possible ways of sharing them.

Revelation of itself may not always be edifying. All knowledge is not necessarily good. Its source may be deceptive. The Bible spells out carefully that there is a source of forbidden knowledge that neither man nor woman may tap. Basically, the fall of man depicted in Genesis 3 was over a desire to become wise by doing that which was forbidden:

> But of the tree of the knowledge of good and evil you shall not eat, for in the day that you eat of it you shall surely die (Gen. 2:17).

> The secret things belong to the LORD our God, but those things which are revealed belong to us and to our children forever (Deut. 29:29).

> So when the woman saw that the tree was good for food, that it was pleasant to the eyes, and a tree desirable to make one wise, she took of its fruit and ate. She also gave to her husband with her, and he ate. Then the eyes of both of them were opened (Gen. 3:6,7).

Anxiety of the Faithful

It is perfectly natural for Bible-loving Christians to be concerned on finding that some of their brothers in Christ are wanting to introduce the revelatory gifts of the Spirit into the worship and ministry of the church. This is especially likely to be the case where those claiming to have the gifts are perceived as the lunatic fringe and are not in fact well integrated with or committed to the local body of Christ; or when the prophet is somebody everyone knows could easily take leave of the fellowship tomorrow, even if slightly offended.

But there are two other reasons why such endeavors will encounter stout opposition in the church. One is the total unfamiliarity that many Christians have with anything of the kind. There has been no history of exposure to such manifestations in a wholesome environment (under authority and in a climate where prophecy may be properly weighed and tested), nor have most of them had any positive biblical teaching on the subject; indeed usually the very opposite is true.

The other reason is that any unfamiliar experience of the supernatural seems "spooky." There is genuine fear and suspicion that anything of this nature could be an "apparently" biblical and subtle disguise for introducing occult influences into the worship and ministry of the church. Evil "New Age" teaching is already surreptitiously insinuating itself even into the church, just like the "Old Age" practices insinuated themselves into the very holy temple of Israel (Ezek. 8). The church can never relax her watch. There is a constant need to be wise and vigilant.

In any situation where someone believes he has a message from a supernatural source (a hot line from God) and declares it to the community, there is always the possibility that this could be counterfeit. False prophets were the bane of Israel as they have been of the church down the ages. We know we must be discerning about the source of revelation.

Sharing Revelations

We must also be very careful of the way that we use revelation. Jesus was quite specific about this and frequently explained to the disciples how he worked together with his Father. Christians who operate with revelatory gifts should bear the following four points in mind:

1. Jesus only did and said *what* he heard the Father saying and doing (John 5:19).

123

2. Jesus only said what the Father said and only said it *how* the Father wanted him to say it (John 12:49). There are certainly counterproductive ways of saying what we sense God is saying. Paul had this in mind, I think, when he wrote about "speaking the truth in love" (Eph. 4:15).

3. Jesus only said and did things *when* the Father told him, and not before (John 16:12). Even though Mary was his own mother, Jesus resisted her pressing appeal for instant intervention at the wedding in Cana of Galilee (John 2:3,4); and He delayed after the urgent emotional pleas of his two friends, Martha and Mary, on the occasion of Lazarus' terminal sickness (John 11:3–6), because the time was not yet right.

4. At times, it seems, things were revealed to Jesus that he never shared (John 16:12). It is not always necessary to communicate a revelation from God. Its purpose may simply be a pointer for prayer or a guide for helping someone in need.

Prudence is Called For

Clearly any revealed knowledge must be shared with wisdom and restraint and always "in love"—putting ourselves in the other people's shoes and sensing just how we would feel in their place. There is the temptation (arising especially if we are ambitious or insecure) to use revelation insensitively in the rush to notch up for ourselves some kind of extra points!

Bob Jones, a prophet of maturity, tells how the Lord showed him the impending downfall of Jimmy Swaggart which would be made public on February 17, 1988. Bob shared this revelation with some of his friends. Finally the day came and Bob became very excited. "We got it—we were right on target! Jimmy Swaggart has fallen." In the following days there was a tremendous public outcry against TV evangelists. Swaggart's name was mud. Christians were portrayed as one great bunch of hypocrites. The Lord's name was shamed.

Bob Jones tells how after a while the Lord took him on one side and rebuked him. "That is one of my sons you were talking about—one of my sons I love has fallen and you seem pleased about it! How would you feel if people went around talking about one of your sons who had fallen from grace and caused you great shame? You should have mourned and not rejoiced."

The Lord rebuked Bob for his spiritual pride and warned him that he would withdraw the gift from him if he misused it again. Bob was silenced and hastily withdrew to his woodshed to repent. He was very humble about it and said he wished he had had the wisdom of Paul Cain, who wept before the Lord when Swaggart's final downfall had come about with all the media publicity. Bob told this story to help us avoid the pitfalls he had fallen into.

The young Joseph—that dreamer—did not share his revelations very wisely at the beginning; this aggravated his brothers, who rejected him, and embarrassed his father Jacob, who rebuked him (Gen. 37:5–11). The revelations were absolutely true and their interpretations later fulfilled on a grand scale, but he lacked prudence in sharing them. It seems that the real value of the revelation was for Joseph himself, to sustain him during his hidden prison years in exile, and possibly they were never intended to be shared with anyone else anyway.

II. Interpretation

Revelations from the Lord need to be wisely handled. Often they can be quite difficult to understand. Sometimes they cannot be understood because significant events have not yet taken place.

Soon after George Bush was nominated for president in 1988 by the Republican party, one of the Kansas City prophets had an enigmatic "word" concerning him, which none of them could understand. It was a kind of riddle—one of those dark sayings the Bible talks about (Num. 12:8, Ps. 78:2, 1 Cor. 13:12).

Bush was reported to be out hunting on vacation at the time. The "word" was "Bush is hunting quail and the quail is behind the bush!" It was not till a few weeks later that Bush nominated his choice of vice-presidential candidate—Dan Quayle—as his running mate in the forthcoming election; a nomination that came as a complete surprise to just about everyone.

This was a typical case of what seemed to be an obscure or improbable "word" being proved in an unexpected way. So much will depend upon the interpretation and the interpretation will depend upon so much. The person who gets the revelation does not always understand the interpretation. Neither the butler nor the baker nor Pharaoh could interpret their own dreams: only Joseph was able to do that.

Before any revelation (at the level we see in the earlier chapters) is communicated to the church, it is vital to share the vision first with the leadership and let them help with the interpretation.

Some people interpret out of their gifting; others interpret out of their office, just like any other ministry for the Lord—healing, for example. As there is a gift of interpretation for tongues so there is a gift for revelations which both Joseph and Daniel quite clearly had: "Take me before the king, and I will tell the king the interpretation," said Daniel (Dan. 2:24).

Problems arise when enthusiastic Christians operating out of their own bias allow this to distort both their revelations and interpretations. In no way, however, am I saying that simply because a man has had a limited education he should be disqualified from either an authentic revelation or a valid interpretation. I think the case of Bob Jones proves that point.

At the Kansas City Fellowship they have a strict rule about bringing the prophecy to the leadership so that both prophets and pastors can consider it, provided the person submitting their prophecy comply with one basic requirement. (Mike came up with this practice because he found that people frequently unloaded their prophecies on him verbally while hand-shaking after the Sunday night service. He would go to bed confused and by Monday morning was certainly none the wiser!)

Mike requires his flock to type out in full any prophecy that they wish him to receive. They must then summarize the gist of it in a few lines on another clean page and add their name, phone number, and the date. (Glancing at a recent but still unread letter containing some kind of prophecy handwritten across five large pieces of paper, which will take me some time to read, I find this rule a welcome one.) Having given the prophecy to the leadership the hands of the sender are now clean. The responsibility is with the leadership. They will call if they want further elucidation.

If there are a number of independent prophecies all saying much the same thing then the leadership should pick up the drift of what God is saying easily enough when there is a real openness to the direction of the Holy Spirit.

It will not help if the sender begins to share his prophecy with others and then starts counting heads to further waylay and convince the minister. He will then be less inclined to see it as a word from the Lord and more inclined to regard it as the work of a pressure group impatient with the Lord.

There is a real need for careful and prayerful interpretation. This may be seen from the following example, again from the KCF. One of the "prophets" plainly recognized the face of a member of the fellowship in his vision. He proceeded to accuse the man he had seen of being a fraud. The man confronted flatly denied there was any truth in the accusation. Mike Bickle now began to question the "prophet" very closely.

"I swear I saw his face and recognized this man," said the prophet.

"And what else did you see that made you think he was involved in fraud?" asked Mike.

"I saw his head in a big cloud and there were dollar signs on the cloud!" said the prophet.

Eventually it became clear that the reason the man's head was depicted as being in the clouds was because something was happening concerning him which he knew nothing about; it was all veiled from his sight. The prophet agreed that this could well be part of the interpretation. The dollar signs seemed to indicate it had to do with money. It could mean that there was some kind of financial misdeed going on somewhere which this brother needed to know about, but of which he was obviously still completely ignorant. This eventually turned out to be the case. After full investigation of the books some serious embezzlement by one of the partners in his business was uncovered. But for the very careful interpretation with the help of the pastor this might never have come to light. The great embarrassment over the confrontation gave way to thankful acknowledgment for the revelation.

Many prophets think they should be left to interpret their own revelations. Those with some experience in these things think that, generally speaking, it is best otherwise. In the multitude of counselors there is wisdom.

III. Application

This is what we should do with the prophecy and its interpretation. Many practical questions arise here. Should the whole church be told or just a few members? Now or later? How much of the prophecy? All of it or part? Mike Bickle says that at first they shared the whole prophecy with the whole congregation—

even when they still did not understand much of it. This quickly became totally unprofitable. Many of the symbols were unintelligible and the parables and enigmas insoluble. The bottom line in the operation of the gifts must be the common good (1 Cor. 12:7). Sharing the whole prophecy to the whole congregation was clearly not ministering to the common good in their situation. In fact, it soon became very counterproductive and aroused hostility towards any kind of prophecy.

They now rarely tell the whole congregation anything until there is a reason to do so—that is, when the Lord has clearly led them to take some action for the common good that the congregation needs to know about.

For instance, when Noel Alexander joined the staff they were able to share with the church how the Lord had led them to take him on, starting with Bob's strange word to Mike at one of the prayer meetings when he blurted out, "The Lord says Noel is coming!" Had they shared that with the congregation initially it would doubtless have left everyone both bemused and confused.

Most revelation of this kind is simply to confirm some individual's personal direction by God or to enlighten someone in his personal intercessions for others. Many of the prophecies given to the leaders were meant for the leaders personally. This was John Wimber's testimony regarding the immense help he was given from Paul Cain, living in Dallas, during a 1988 leadership crisis at Anaheim on the West Coast.

Prophets may be led to share other prophecies with other individual members in the congregation privately, provided the leadership does not object. This was the case in the story we have already told about Bob Jones, who revealed things to Art Katz that led to blessing on a much wider front and eventually included Mike Bickle himself.

RESTORING THE PROPHETIC MINISTRY TO THE CHURCH

A small conference on prophecy was advertised for the end of April 1987. It was to be held in Birmingham, Alabama. Mike Bickle was booked as the main speaker, and several of the prophets from Kansas City went along with him. One of those attending was Paul Cain, someone we know Mike had long wanted to meet. Whether those from Kansas City knew that Paul Cain would be present is not clear, but Paul certainly knew that Mike Bickle would be there since his name had been advertised on the program. At one point during the conference the host suggested to Mike that it might seem appropriate to invite Paul to say a few words to the rest of the conference, whereupon Paul came forward to prophesy. His words were all directed towards the Kansas City team. What they heard astounded them.

Everything that their local prophets had already been sharing among themselves about revival breaking out in Kansas City and spreading to the far corners of the earth was being confirmed to them in this almost incredible way. It had to be God! They just knew it. By the end of the prophecy the whole party from Kansas City was on the floor weeping before the Lord.

After the meeting was over they introduced themselves to

Paul Cain, initiating a warm friendship which has since flourished. It was only natural that they should invite him to Kansas City, and Paul visited them on May 10–12.

A Dark Saying

Prior to his visit the KCF had been seeking and praying about a new center for worship, because their old meeting hall, which seated 700, was no longer big enough. One of the prophets had been given a vision of the new place and the detail which impressed everyone was that there appeared to be a lot of green grass involved with it; the prophet said he definitely saw green grass!

This was quite obviously another of those "dark sayings" that God sometimes gives his people to puzzle and pray over. Some thought it implied that the building would be on a street with a name that could naturally be associated with "green grass"—perhaps "Grassways" or "Meadow Lane"! Others felt it must have something to do with a new building on ground that at the moment was still grassed over! It really was a teaser and they had a lot of fun trying to figure it all out.

One day Mike had a visit from a couple of Christian businessmen who owned a sports complex on Grandview Road. The complex was not going very well and they wanted to sell it. They had felt that if there was any Christian concern that was interested they would be willing to sell cheaply and so help the Lord's work.

They suggested to Mike that he should take a look at it. Before doing this he needed to verify that the place could actually hold 5,000 people. Mike was remembering other prophecies with regard to that number. He also made sure there was permission from the fire department and others for seating so many.

He then took some of his leadership team round to see the

place. As soon as they got there they knew that these must be the premises God had planned for them. The floor was covered with a carpet of artificial grass—a surface required for the athletic events and the ball games which had been held there. The deal was negotiated quickly and they were soon in. The green grass flooring is still there, not only looking fresh and pleasant but as a constant reminder of God's wonderful leading and provision.

Joel's Army Training Center

By the time Paul Cain arrived in Kansas City the fellowship was well settled into their new meeting place at the Grandview Worship Center. Paul immediately recognized the location from the crossroads outside as the place which the Lord had showed him many times (possibly twenty, over as many years) as a spiritual training center for the soldiers of Joel's army that God was raising up for the coming revival.

"Many years ago," said Paul, "I came to the crossroads of life and I saw a vision of an illuminated billboard on which was written: 'Joel's army in training.' It was on these crossroads with an arrow pointing to this spot—though there was no building on it then! I believe God has shown me that here he is going to raise up an army. This army is not a destructive army but a deliverance army. God is not going to work in a major way through superstar Christians any more, but through ordinary soldiers who will hear God's spirit in the midst of this Laodicean age which is rampaging the Church. These soldiers will be genuine 'Jesus' people. They will need to strip themselves for service. There is no Mickey-Mouse religion for them.

"The Lord is raising up a new breed of Christians who will not be looking for their own glory. A new breed of leaders and teachers is coming—Joel's army—who will be working for the glory of God. Many years ago the American Indians used to go through the forests in single file. Each Indian would put his moccasin in the step of the man in front of him. The enemy would see the footprint and say an Indian had passed that way. They never realized it was a large fighting force. In the days to come, when the blind see, the deaf hear, and the lame walk, the people will no longer say, 'Kathryn Kuhlman passed this way today' or 'Reinhardt Bonnke passed this way today.' No, they will say 'Jesus passed this way today!' There will be no other footprints, only the footprints of Jesus who alone will have all the glory.''

Although Paul had actually seen a vision of this spot many times, he was fearful about visiting it in case he found men and women there of the wrong spirit. When he heard Mike Bickle's message about new wineskins in preparation for the coming revival his heart was warmed. When he recognized the seriousness of God's calling upon them, the simplicity of their lifestyles, their discipline in fasting and intercession, their yearning after holiness, and their care for the poor he was deeply moved. It was an exciting confirmation for Paul to discover at last the actual place he had seen so often in his vision, and also for Mike to have the added assurance of God's purposes for the Kansas City Fellowship; Mike and the leadership certainly and sincerely wanted Jesus to have all the glory.

Those two days with Paul Cain were mutually beneficial in other ways also. There was great blessing through Paul Cain's public ministry to the fellowship. But the discovery of the Kansas City Fellowship was a blessing to Paul Cain as well.

Ministry to Leaders

We have already referred to Paul's health. He was obviously not well and was having considerable heart problems. This may have been partly attributable to the particular kind of stressful

ministry he had had. Every now and then Paul was led by God
to seek out a leader privately, either a spiritual one, an indus-
trialist, or a politician. Often the revelations were so stunning
and the warnings so serious that the recipients would become
quite offensive. Sometimes, like the woman of Samaria who
said, "Come, see a Man who told me all things that I ever
did" (John 4:29)—a slight exaggeration to say the least—the recipients would mistakenly assume that because Paul had been
shown some things very clearly he must therefore know everything!

Like many other prophets before him Paul Cain has had threats
on his life because of this. He has never altogether shaken off
the possibility that he might one day meet a grizzly end at the
hands of the Mafia or some other mercenary. Not a pleasant
prospect! Who would be a prophet?

It is easy to see how this lonely kind of ministry can take its
toll. Paul was increasingly concerned about the lack of intercessory prayer backing he would have once his aged mother passed
on; she was over 104 and could not live forever. He was very
dependent on her for her committed spiritual support. Where
could he ever hope to get such sympathetic and understanding
coverage as that which she provided for him through her intercessions and communion with the Lord? Wherever would he look
for the kind of wise and godly counsel she had given him all
his life?

An answer to all this was slowly becoming plain to Mike
Bickle. After praying about it he felt led to invite Paul to come
up from Dallas and join the team in Kansas City, should anything
happen to his mother. For this Paul is profoundly grateful though
if he goes, his route will be via California to spend time close
to the Christian Vineyard Fellowship currently at Anaheim. Members of the Kansas City Fellowship are already committed to
interceding for Paul. Those who know him say that his health

has already improved markedly and his ministry increased powerfully.

There is even a project afoot there, in response to prophecy, to set up a kind of sanctuary near Kansas City for five or six members of the prophetic team and their families. It will be called Shiloh. Since it is expected that the team will be increasingly involved in travel it is intended to become a shelter for restoration of their physical health, spiritual vitality, and emotional well-being, and to protect them from the urgency and demands of their ministries. It will definitely not be a "visitors' center."

Paul Cain and John Wimber Meet

John Wimber had his first encounter with Mike Bickle in 1985, and this was a very positive meeting for both of them. By 1988 he was increasingly aware of the prophetic ministry being exercised at the Kansas City Fellowship, where Mike was the leading pastor. Some of his Vineyard Christian Fellowship pastors were reporting back on the KCF very favorably. In October that year John Wimber invited Mike Bickle to accompany him on a ministry tour to the United Kingdom. Five days before John called him, Bob Jones, following a divine revelation, told Mike that John Wimber would soon be contacting him and that this would open a wide door for Mike's future ministry.

In the autumn of that same year Paul Cain sensed the Lord telling him to go and see John Wimber in California. Jack Deere, an intermediary for Paul in Dallas, phoned and asked for an appointment. Though extremely grateful for his help at a critical time earlier in the year, John was under pressure and was not too keen on the idea of meeting Paul. Jack urged John to make a special effort since Paul felt such a meeting was very important for both of them. Paul would accept any time that was convenient.

Eventually John was able to dig out five dates to offer him in December. Jack Deere thanked him and said Paul would book the second one. "By the way," he added, "so that you will know that God has a strategic purpose in this for Paul and the Vineyard movement, Paul says there will be an earthquake that day!"

Jack had asked Paul if it was going to be a big earthquake. Paul had replied, "No, but a big earthquake will occur elsewhere in the world on the day after I leave."

As John Wimber commented when we were over there later, "To predict an earthquake for southern California is no big deal—we do get them here—but to predict the exact date for an earthquake so far ahead has to be significant."

And there was an earthquake in California, as Paul had predicted, on the very day he arrived! Paul did not say where the earthquake would be on the day he left California; but there was in fact a terrible one on December 7, 1988, the day he left. It was in Armenia and was reported worldwide.

When Paul finally met John Wimber he was surprised. For a couple of years he had been searching for the Christian leader God had told him about who would give him a platform to use for the restoration of the prophetic ministry to the church. Somehow he had never imagined that John Wimber could be that man. John was too busy with the vision God had given him and would be in too much demand to cope with Paul's vision and particular call from God—so Paul Cain seems to have rationalized.

Now that they had met, Paul was able to minister to John* all that God had laid on his heart for him. Paul was greatly moved at the open and humble way John received him. Then,

---

* See Wimber's account of the effect of that visit upon him in his publication *Equipping the Saints*, Fall, 1989.

quite clearly, the Lord told Paul that this was the man he had been raising up to use his platform for the restoration of the prophetic ministry in the church.

Complaining to John Wimber

Mary and I had flown on to California to stay a couple of days to meet John and Carol Wimber, at their kind invitation. This was about five months after their own linkup with Paul and we had not had a chance to discuss it. There was so much to talk to them about after our mind-blowing weekend in Kansas City. It was good to be able to relax with friends. We certainly had some thoughts to ventilate to them—especially since John had been the one who originally introduced this level of prophetic ministry to us through Mike Bickle. Then there was a possibility that John might one day introduce Paul Cain to Britain.

"How could one really ever sponsor that kind of thing?" I asked John.

We mentioned Paul's style of preaching which had concerned us. Probably, I think, what worried us most was the reaction our evangelical friends in England would have should they ever hear Paul preach.

I said, "Do you know that when he got up to preach that evening he announced a verse that he said the Lord had impressed upon him some seven different ways. I thought to myself that this must be going to be a good sermon; he's really got a burden for it! He gave us the biblical reference for the verse but then he never read it or preached from it! Can you believe it?" I shook my head sadly at the memory of such a letdown!

John glanced towards me. "Did you look it up?"

"No!" I said, "It never occurred to me to do that because he went on to preach about something else!"

"Well, I imagine that was what you were meant to do," said John simply.

"Of course," I thought, "what a fool I have been. Why did I never think of looking it up?"

I thought I had better be careful about airing my other doubts too readily after that. I did not mention my problem with Paul's obvious Pentecostal theology. It all seemed much less serious as we considered that when God puts his treasures in earthen vessels these vessels will reflect their own earthly views, be they cultural, theological, psychological, emotional, ecclesiastical, or social. Prophets are only human. No matter how impressive the prophet he still only "sees in part." We need to glean from him the purest reflection of his original revelation and then weigh it, sift it, interpret it, and apply it.

But that was not all that I did not share at that time. Another thing that had stuck in my evangelical gullet was a comment made by Paul when he quoted a certain verse of the Bible and said that the King James Version gave the best interpretation of what God really meant concerning that text! "How could a man who was obviously not a linguist," I argued with myself, "say what a text actually meant?"

Even as I was cogitating over this, another question arose within me by way of an answer. Was it not within the realm of possibility that a man who prayed and meditated so long and conscientiously over the Word of God and received such clear revelations from the Lord about present-day situations could be shown what the spirit of God really intended when the original "God-inspired" word was written (2 Tim. 3:16)?

And we could just as easily turn the question around: How could a linguist, who might not have the disciplined devotional life of a man like Paul Cain and had never experienced anything like the revelations that Paul had, necessarily claim to have a better understanding of what God really meant in certain debatable passages? Obviously no prophet could distort Scripture to mean something incompatible with the text or contrary to the plain teaching of the rest of Scripture. Indeed, the prophet himself must subject all his own insights and revelations to the Word of God for testing. But a prophet might sometimes have better insights than the experts! Prophecy and teaching are distinctive ministries to help get the balance right.

There seemed no doubt that the prophets we had met were humble, kindly, generous, godly, and dedicated men and women of prayer. They deferred to Mike Bickle, their leader, and to one another in a truly beautiful way. They really loved the Lord and studied his Word. Though we had left them with many questions still on our lips and with more that were still to surface, we had to admit that we really liked these people and they were good to be with. One felt oneself thirsting after righteousness, living and worshipping among them. We had to admit that it certainly seemed that they were receiving prophecies at a high level of revelation and these were being confirmed with remarkable signs.

We had certainly never seen anything like this before, and that was in spite of many years working in Chile where we had observed Pentecostalism firsthand. We had met many strange things there, such as people (even in our own churches) having their teeth miraculously filled (*creatio ex nihilo*), but we had never come across anything quite like this high level of prophecy out there.

Every now and again we heard of prophecies being fulfilled to the letter but they were usually single occurrences. A woman once foretold a major earthquake in central Chile in May 1960, but to the best of our knowledge she did not have a prophetic ministry that was verifiably sustained over a prolonged period. Indeed, we certainly had no idea that it was possible to find such a prophetic ministry being exercised in a Christian church anywhere in the world today, though there seems no obvious reason from the Bible why this should not be the case.

A Paradigm Shift

We felt we were experiencing a paradigm shift—we were beginning to see another way of looking at the foundational things we held dear, without having in any way to discard them. Perhaps that is what the Bible meant when it spoke about scales falling from Paul's eyes. Some professed Christians have discarded the Bible on the grounds that they could not believe the Lord had revealed himself throughout history in the ways the biblical writers depicted. We have never had any real problem with that.

But what about revelations today? And why now after all these centuries? And so late in one's ministry! And why was it that Americans seemed to have the "hot lines" to God? John and Carol doubtless had their own answers to similar questions and others, but when we were through they turned to look at each other in obvious amusement and laughed. They felt they had just listened to a complete replay from our lips of objections with which they too had struggled.

It was by no means the first time in their ministry that they had encountered a dilemma of this kind. They could not forget the first time in 1980 when the spirit of God had fallen with great and unaccustomed power upon the Vineyard they were pastoring in Orange County, California. Not knowing what to make of all the associated phenomenology, John had stayed up all night searching the Scriptures, praying, and looking up the history of revivals. Very early the next morning, still uncertain what to make of it all, he had had a long-distance phone call from a friend in Denver, who said that God had given him a message for John when he was praying for him early that morning. He could not understand what it meant, he said. It was simply

God saying something like, "It's all right, John. That was ME!"
How often since then have I heard John himself say, "Why
can't we just let God be God." Sometimes it can be very difficult
but sooner or later we have to adjust to the fact that he is
sovereign and can do what he likes, how he likes, and when
he likes.

What Should We Think?

So how do we conclude? Is there going to be a restoration of
the prophetic ministry to the church? Are we going to see revival
on a grand scale? Will there be persecutions? Are we really
living in the end times?

In spite of the tragic claims through the ages of some who
have sincerely but mistakenly believed themselves to be prophets,
I do not see any problem in believing that, from a biblical perspec-
tive, this could be a very genuine prophetic ministry which, in
accordance with God's will, is being restored to the church today.
After all, Paul deals succinctly with the gift of prophecy in
1 Corinthians 14:3, clearly seeing it as a gift for the church.
He also reminds the readers in his Ephesians letter (4:8–11)
that Jesus, *after his ascension*, gave gifts to men. Among those
post-ascension gifts there was prophecy. Prophets may have been
frustrated and persecuted, but the gift should never again be
denied nor prophecy forbidden its proper place in the ordered
life of the church. This is not to say that prophets of this kind
are meant to take up much time at gatherings for public worship
for reasons already explained elsewhere.

Prophecy of this revelatory kind does not have to be regarded
as a pre-Christian thing. But too many "prophets" have simply
pretended to have the gift or used it counterproductively and
there is little credibility for such "prophets" today. Also too
often critics have behaved badly towards the prophet—consider-
ing the superficial directives recommended in the early days of

the primitive Church in the *Didache*—down to the discounting of all such revelatory prophecy today or the branding of all prophecy as occult. These latter negative approaches are very crushing to anyone just beginning to receive revelations from God. The holy gift is threatened with strangulation at birth.

The kind of prophecy we have mentioned in this book is not in fact quite such an affront to the intellect because it is delivered with the promise of accompanying signs, the fulfillment of which enhances credibility.

Persecution and the "End Time" Overtones

When the early church began to be persecuted (Acts 5) the disciples were soon dispersed abroad. As this happened the church grew. This constituted a threat to the state and the persecution consequently spread and intensified. There is no reason to believe we should be spared persecution if revival comes again on the grand scale foretold by the Old Testament prophets. Indeed, the New Testament endorses this view (Matt. 24:9–14; Rev. 13:14–17).

Finally, the "latter days" element of these prophecies needs to be looked at fairly and squarely since this has been one of the common features in so many of the false prophecies down the ages. (Some examples of this were spelled out in chapter 1.) But in this case, though there have been prophecies about the last days and the Laodicean age for the church, no dates have ever been set for the Lord's return by these Kansas City prophets, nor would we believe they would ever do anything so foolish. They are far too well grounded in Scripture to be so deceived. We cannot discount them for seeing their prophecies in terms of "the last days" because it is possible that these are indeed the end times.

In one sense we have been living in the last days ever since

God finally spoke to us through his Son (Heb. 1:2), but there have to be days that are imminent to those days before the Lord's eventual second coming. We could well be living in those lawless days now.

The prophecy of Joel was wisely quoted by Peter in Acts 2 as relevant, but it is obvious that Pentecost was only a partial fulfillment of Joel 2:28. It still awaits the last days when the Spirit will come in some fresh and final way, and our sons and daughters will prophesy.

We are almost on the threshold of a new millennium—the year 2000 whose coming will provide a major "time mark" in history and an obvious impetus for preachers of all kinds to focus on the end times; yet these days in which we live may still prove to be the last days. No one can possibly demonstrate that these prophets are wrong to talk in this way because only the future can reveal who is right in this matter. There are good grounds, as we have seen, for thinking that these prophets are being faithful to the Lord in speaking out as they do. They sincerely believe God is showing them things that are to happen in the last days. They give signs quite beyond man's ability to manipulate as backup for their predictions. Plenty of people have been wrong about this before and have made fools of themselves by fixing dates in plain contradiction of Scripture. Even as I wrote this, a group of fundamentalist Christians were expecting the Rapture to happen that very same week! How wrong they were!

Someone Must be Right Someday

Sooner or later someone will have to be right about the proximity of the last days, although no one would ever be right to predict actual dates (Acts 1:7). The last days are certainly coming. Jesus himself taught about them (Matt. 24) in terms of the conclusion

143

of the age. This age itself is the last temporal era (Heb. 1:2). The last days of the last age could be here soon but, before they come, Jesus said that "this gospel of the kingdom will be preached in all the world as a witness to all nations, and then the end will come" (Matt. 24:14). The end of the era will not come before every nation has heard the good news and then Christ will come again. That's how the church has always understood it! That is how we must understand it now and that is how it will surely be! As John Wimber has indicated in his lectures on prophecy at Holy Trinity Church, Brompton, London (1990), "Even if we are mistaken in believing that Christ's coming is near, we will have lost nothing for such a mistake. We will have been much better off for having embraced the standards of 'holy conduct and godliness' (2 Peter 3:11–12) and having earnestly sought Christ's coming."

Since beginning to write this book, reports have appeared in both the religious and secular press (see *Christian Newsworld*, December 1989, and the *Evening Standard* [London] November 25, 1989) that the astronaut James Erwin has flown by helicopter over a particular site on the borders of Turkey with Armenia and claimed that the remains of the ark have been located. We await fuller reports. Revival too is reported to have broken out in Armenia recently. This was also part of Bob Jones's prophecy connected with the finding of Noah's ark mentioned in the original introduction to this book.

The fulfillment of each sign is a further encouragement that the other predictions emanating from Kansas City and Paul Cain concerning widespread revival are about to come to pass. Time will tell. Furthermore it would seem that the promises about the restoration of the prophetic office through the church (the corporate Elijah) will become a renewed spiritual reality in evangelism to prepare the world for the glorious second coming of Christ and the awesome Day of Judgment.

AFTERWORD

Evaluating the New "Prophecy Movement"

The ancient Greeks thought the words of a poet were the words of the gods spoken through the lips of a man.

Many of the Hebrew prophets used poetry when prophesying, but their means—unlike the Greeks—were never looked upon as the end. The message, not the messenger, was the only thing that counted.

While the Greeks immortalized language ("the Greeks have a word for it"), the Hebrews struggled with the application of the *word* into their lives and their society. God spoke through the prophets and he expected—indeed, demanded—a response.

The biblical prophets did far more than predict the future. Most were *forth*tellers rather than *fore*tellers. Many pulpiteers have the prophetic ministry of *forth*telling. But recently the ministry of *fore*telling has reached a new prominence.

The newest emphasis in the kingdom is on the emergence of prophets and prophetic utterances. Because of the emphasis of the charismatic movement over the last twenty-five years, most Christians (even Christian leaders) believe God is *still* speaking and that prophets are his mouthpiece. Now, however, the prophetic ministry has been thrust into the forefront—and with it has come the always-attending controversy.

In 1989 *Charisma* magazine devoted an entire issue to the emerging prophetic ministry. Special attention was given to the various prophets and prophecies coming out of Mike Bickle and his Kansas City Fellowship. Shortly afterward John Wimber picked up the prophetic baton and began running strongly. His huge Bible conferences featured many of the prophets from the Kansas City Fellowship and drew thousands, with many more thousands being turned away for lack of space.

Then, without warning, a bombshell exploded. Ernie Gruen, a respected Kansas City pastor, led the dissenting voices raised against the extremes of prophetic movement. Most of the objections were solid, pointing out errors that desperately needed correction.

The controversy concerned the prophetic ministry of KCF—particularly Bickle and an older prophet, Bob Jones. It began when Gruen issued serious charges in a widely distributed tape entitled, "Do We Keep Smiling and Say Nothing?" Gruen has long been looked upon as one of the fathers of the charismatic movement in Kansas City. His large, well-established Full Faith Church is the hub of several smaller satellite bodies around the perimeter of the city.

In his emotion-packed message, Gruen accused KCF of sending out false prophets, of prophesying area churches to close down (and then join KCF), and of outright lying. "A prophet who admits he is right only 40 percent of the time is not only a nonprophet," Gruen charged, "he is dangerous."

Following the release of his tape, more than forty Kansas City pastors contacted Gruen saying they agreed with his position. Gruen was now thrust into the role of chief prosecutor of the movement.

Heresy Trial Requested

In April, Gruen proposed to the Network of Christian Ministries that he and Bickle bring the dispute before their Board of Governors—a group of twelve leaders from some of the nation's independent ministries. Gruen's proposal would have forced that board into the unenviable and dangerous position of an apostolic council—something charismatics have violently opposed in years past.

In May, Bickle was invited by the Charismatic Concerns Committee to attend their annual retreat near St. Louis. He was well received, but he refused to discuss Gruen or his accusations.

Others, however, were not so gracious. Several pastors, having heard Gruen's tape, preached sermons warning their people to stay away from any "prophecy conference." Pat Robertson aired some of the problems on a broadcast with Dick Mills on "The 700 Club." The controversy was heating up.

Vineyard Christian Fellowship Steps

In May 1990, KCF churches submitted themselves to John Wimber's Vineyard Christian Fellowship and became Vineyard Churches. In a personal letter to me Wimber wrote:

> Both Mike Bickle and the prophetic ministries represented by these congregations have submitted themselves to my spiritual authority and oversight. . . . I have made a careful investigation of abuses and errors, both in pastoral ministry and prophetic ministry. While I have not personally found any of Ernie Gruen's charges to be substantiated, I have found certain excesses and errors that required both discipline and correction. I have taken the necessary steps to institute both discipline and correction in this matter. Mike Bickle and the individual prophetic ministries have submitted to the discipline and correction, and I am satisfied that we will not see these problems arising again in the future.

Wimber also wrote the Network board saying it was best for him to handle the problems rather than having a heresy trial. The board members I talked to expressed great relief that they were not going to have to preside over a heresy trial.

Gruen, however, released a 233-page spiral-bound document listing numerous charges against KCF. Most of the document was composed of excerpts from taped messages—particularly messages by Bickle, Paul Cain, and Bob Jones, whose prophecies seemed to be at the heart of the issue. Bickle and Cain immediately requested a meeting with Gruen and the board of the National Leadership Conference (NLC) which was then in session. Cain said Gruen was being unfair by printing accusations against him without first contacting him. They urged him to withhold distribution of the book until Wimber could examine the issues. As president of the NLC board I called a meeting at Ridgecrest, North Carolina, and we strongly urged Gruen—who was an NLC board member—to consider their request. Cain said he was flying to Kansas City and would sit and wait until Gruen talked to him. Gruen refused to withdraw the book, but he did agree to a private meeting with Cain and Wimber.

The outcome of that Memorial Day weekend meeting totally changed the direction of the controversy. Gruen, who later called it a "sweet meeting in the Spirit," opened by saying, "I do not have war in my heart." Wimber and Cain said they only wanted God's best. The result was the issuance of a joint statement to all factions saying the opposing leaders trusted each other's integrity and spirit and wanted to model for the nation a "righteous method" of handling disputes.

Personal Conclusions

In the meantime, the movement continued to grow. During that time I drew several conclusions:

- God is indeed speaking, and prophets are his mouthpiece.
- People are hungry to hear from God and will travel great distances in hopes of hearing him speak, if not to them then to someone else.
- People are lazy and would rather have someone tell them what God is saying than go to him personally—which is still the best way.
- Sensationalism draws huge crowds. As people came to see miracles—or a sideshow at a carnival—so they will come to hear prophecy.
- If "prophecy" only tells you (and others eagerly listening in) what you have in the left-hand pocket of your coat or what you did on your thirteenth birthday, it is worthless. Check: it may be ESP rather than a word from God.
- The "prophecy movement" carries with it the seeds of deception. At worst in the "discipleship/shepherding movement," some shepherd told you what to do. In the "prophecy movement," it's God (?) who tells you what to do.
- All prophecy, public and personal, should be submitted to (1) local leadership and (2) other prophets for confirmation.
- The "prophecy movement" desperately needs moderation and balance to keep it in the mainstream of God's work.
- It's easier to hear God through a "prophet" than it is through your spouse.

Judging Prophecy

Personal prophecy—that is, prophets who either come to you personally or single you out in a public meeting and deliver "words"—is at the heart of this new movement.

The problem lies in discerning who is a prophet and who is not, as well as which prophecies are true and which are false.

Years ago Derek Prince told me the only way to determine

if futuristic prophecy was true or false was to wait and see if it came to pass. That's wisdom.

Also, those who receive personal prophecy must remember that it should never be used for guidance—only for confirmation. Brother Andrew once told me some real horror stories coming out of the early days of Bible smuggling in Europe. Prophets had told his Dutch smugglers that God would blind the eyes of Communist border guards when the smugglers went through the checkpoint into eastern Europe carrying Bibles in their car. As a result the young missionaries did not hide the Bibles as they ordinarily would have. The border guards detained them when they saw the Bibles. The vehicle was confiscated and the young missionaries were arrested. They had used the prophecy for guidance rather than confirmation.

Many years ago a South African prophet by the name of Thomm, who was being promoted by Pat Robertson, singled me out in a meeting. He knew I was a book and magazine writer, but knew nothing else. Pointing his finger at me he said I would write twenty books and would be asked to become editor of the Full Gospel Businessman's *Voice* magazine. "Do not accept that position," he warned. I took this as a "word" that I was to keep on writing. I've written twice that number of books, but I never was even considered, to my knowledge, as editor of *Voice*. However, had I been offered the job, accepted it, and later regretted the decision, I couldn't blame God.

On the other hand, Paul was warned by Agabus not to return to Jerusalem. If he did, the prophet said, he would be bound in chains (see Acts 21:10 ff.). Paul felt his call overrode the prophecy, went to Jerusalem, was bound in chains, and never was free from arrest from that time until his death. Should he have obeyed the prophet? The debate will continue forever.

I believe this new move of prophecy is of God; it brings with it what all new moves bring: extremes and extremists. As we evaluate what is happening we need to understand there is a difference between false prophecy and a false prophet. One way to determine a true prophet is his willingness (eagerness) to confess and ask forgiveness for any false prophecy he may have uttered.

Dick Mills of San Jacinto, California, is such a man. Dick entered the prophetic ministry long before most of the modern prophets were born. Recently he sent a letter to Pastor Tom Peters of Trinity Assembly of God in Lake Worth, Florida, dealing with two prophecies he gave while speaking in Tom's church. Neither came to pass.

In his cover letter to me Dick wrote:

> My reason for mailing a copy of this letter to you is because of a strong desire I have to cope with the problem areas that are surfacing in the current focus concerning the prophetic ministries. I feel that all mobile prophetic ministries need to establish accountability as well as credibility. It's my hope this letter can counteract some of the irresponsible things that have happened recently in the body of Christ.

Here is Dick's letter just as it was written.

Dear Pastor Peters and Congregation:

I feel the Lord wants me to write to you all there at Trinity Assembly of God regarding my visit with you in March 1988. At that time I strongly felt a major earthquake was going to happen in the summer months of 1988. I proclaimed it as a prophetic word and now face the fact it did not happen.

In addition to the "Big Bang" word, I also prophesied that Pastor and Mrs. Peters would be out of their house and into another location within 18 months. I even proclaimed an evaluation on the new residence. The 18 months expired and the new house had not materialized. It is obvious that I missed it on both messages, the earthquake and the new home for the Peters.

What are the biblical steps to be taken when traveling ministries

151

visit a congregation and deliver words that do not come to pass? Deuteronomy 18:22 gives us a good sound answer, "If the thing follows not or doesn't come to pass the prophet has spoken it presumptuously, or out of his own spirit."

I'd love to be 100% accurate, but in this situation it has to be a case of human error. One reason I'm writing this letter is because of a desire to be accountable to the Lord, to the church leadership, and to the people.

I answer to three ministers and go to them for corrective words, discipline, and reproof. One of these ministers is Jack Hayford, pastor of Church on the Way. Pastor Hayford made some practical suggestions: Instead of date setting, he recommended I preface my remarks by these words, "In my spirit I feel this could happen," then name the timeframe. This would avoid any statement sounding like an oracle of God or a prophetic word.

Pastor Hayford also suggested that I squarely face the fact that I missed it and not try to come up with anything elusive or evasive. He also felt it was good for the cause of Christ for me to contact you and acknowledge that my own human spirit got in the way of the Holy Spirit.

Not only do I have feet of clay but the clay extends to the top of my head. This is a fact according to 2 Corinthians 4:7 where we have divine treasure in earthen vessels.

I want to apologize for any harm done or any expectations raised that led to disappointment or frustration. I pray you won't give up on prophetic ministry. 1 Thessalonians 5:20–21 says, "Despise not prophecies." We're also told to prove all things and hold fast that which is good. Those very verses let us know that prophecy is valid but needs to be verified. It also implies that we can discriminate between what is to be discarded and what is to be retained.

All of life is a learning process, and I pray we'll all be enriched by this incident and not become embittered.

Releasing the Gift of Prophecy

A friend of mine, Roy Hicks, Jr., offers valuable practical suggestions on releasing the "gifts of the Spirit" into ministry.

1. *Teach.* Don't teach in principle gatherings. Do a series during a midweek gathering. Gifts do not just happen, they are modeled and explained.

2. *Enlist some contenders.* Build the conviction among some of the small group enclaves of your church that you want manifestations of the Spirit. Show up at one of those meetings. Let them hear you pray in earnest.

3. *Wait before the Lord at staff meetings.* Never have a meeting with your principle leaders without waiting before the Lord for some expression of the gifts. If you'll be faithful to do this with them, a pattern will naturally transfer into the larger meetings you lead and into the meetings they lead.

4. *Identify giftedness.* Take time to explain the operation of gifts when they occur. Identify the operation of gifts when they are not readily identifiable—maybe something said in the context of prayer that you recognized as prophetic, or a word of wisdom that was shared in the context of leading in worship. Calmly identify them for the saints without the use of drum rolls and spotlights. We want gifts to become a natural part of our supernatural life.

5. *Make room.* Don't rush. Learn to tarry at the appropriate moment. A pause doesn't require that a prophecy break forth. It is valuable even as silence. You need to give opportunity for gifts to be shared.

6. *Lead the congregation in response.* Never allow a gift to be shared without leading the congregation in some kind of response—either lead a short prayer or ask everyone to repeat quietly what they heard the Lord say to them. Don't simply go on as though nothing happened. That will produce shallowness and an unspoken cynicism about the value of gifts.

7. *Restate.* Ask the person who has shared to repeat what he said, or ask someone else to say what they heard in

the gift. This is especially useful when the style has hindered the content of the gift.

8. *Refer to gifts.* Look for opportunities to use gifts as illustrations in messages or when leading worship. This increases the value of the gift in the congregation's estimation and affirms the one giving the gift.

9. *Use gifts as landmarks.* Jack Hayford sometimes works into a sermon or congregational letter a gift of prophecy that had a shaping impact on the life of the church family or on his own life, even if the prophecy happened years ago.

10. *Link strategies and programs.* Don't be afraid to begin a new church emphasis based on something the Lord said through one of the saints. Look for phrases in prophecies that confirm a direction the church is taking, and point them out to the church.

Although the prophecy controversy will continue on from now until Jesus comes, as long as the leaders involved are people of God, no blood will be shed—and good will come from the tension. I hope people are learning that the basic difference between the Old Testament prophets—who were constantly being stoned—and the New Testament prophets was that the New Testament prophets were part of a team made up of apostles, prophets, evangelists, pastors, and teachers. They submitted their lives—and their prophecies—to each other.

JAMIE BUCKINGHAM

FORBIDDEN COMMUNICATIONS

Scripture Examined

We need to examine Scripture to see which sources man is permitted to communicate with and which not. The Bible is emphatically opposed to man's attempting any communication with the occult (including the dead).

To simplify our understanding of this, there are two particular Hebrew words we need to know, *Ob* and *Yiddeoni*. Following J. Stafford Wright (see below), we take the liberty of forming the plurals for these two unfamiliar Hebrew words by simply adding an "s."

1. *Ob*—the "o" is long and the "b" is pronounced almost like a "v." The King James Authorized Version always translates this word as "familiar spirit," but it can also imply the medium (Lev. 20:27) who is communicating with this familiar or controlling spirit. The precise meaning of *Ob* is uncertain, but a similar word in Arabic means "to return."

2. *Yiddeoni*—the final "o" and "i" are long. In the King

James Authorized Version this is always translated as wizard. *Yiddeoni* is connected with the Hebrew word "to know."

Communicating Spirits

Both words appear to involve a communicating spirit. The main references, from the King James Authorized Version, are

Do not turn to *obs* (mediums) or seek out *yiddeonis* (spiritists) for you will be defiled by them. I am the LORD your God. (Lev. 19:31)

I will set my face [says the Lord] against the person who turns to *obs* (mediums) and *yiddeonis* (spiritists) to prostitute himself by following them, and I will cut him off from his people. (Lev. 20:6)

A man or woman who is an *ob* (medium) or *yiddeoni* (spiritist) among you must be put to death. (Lev. 20:27; cf. also Exod. 22:18)

Let no one be found among you . . . who is an *ob* (medium) or *yiddeoni* (spiritist) or who consults the dead (necromancer). (Deut. 18:10, 11.) This is part of a more comprehensive list of occult practices to be found among the Canaanite inhabitants who were being driven out of the Promised Land.

The nations you will dispossess listen to those who practise sorcery or divination. But as for you, the LORD your God has not permitted you to do so. (Deut. 18:14)

Backsliding Monarchs

Saul had expelled the *obs* (mediums) and the *yiddeonis* (spiritists) from the land (1 Sam. 28:3). Then in his rebellion from God and subsequent desolation he sought out an *ob* (medium).

"Find me a woman who is an *ob* (medium) so that I may go and enquire of her" (1 Sam. 28:7).

They replied, "There is one (an *ob*) in Endor."

Saul ordered the woman to "Consult an *ob* (controlling spirit) . . . and bring up for me the one I name" (1 Sam. 28:8).

This was his crowning act of rebellion against God.

"Saul died because he was unfaithful to the Lord; he did not keep the word of the Lord, and even consulted an *ob* (medium) for guidance, and did not enquire of the Lord. So the Lord put him to death" (1 Chron. 10:13–14).

Saul was not the only king who led God's people astray. Among the list of King Manasseh's sins it is recorded that he used *obs* and *yiddeonis* (2 Kings 21:6; 2 Chron. 33:6).

Reforms Promoted

The reforming king Josiah "got rid of the *obs* (mediums) and *yiddeonis* (spiritists)" (2 Kings 23:24).

Isaiah is relentless in driving home God's law on this detestable practice: "When men tell you to consult *obs* (mediums) and *yiddeonis* (spiritists) who whisper (high pitch) and mutter (low pitch), should not a people enquire of their God? Why consult the dead on behalf of the living? To the law and to the testimony!" (Isa. 8:19–20).

Spiritist Mediums

In *Christianity and the Occult* (from which source I have drawn heavily) J. Stafford Wright, a leading Old Testament scholar of his day, suggests that since in the Bible the word *ob* is sometimes used by itself, whereas *yiddeoni* is always linked with an *ob,* it would be reasonable to suppose that the *ob* is the main control spirit and the *yiddeonis* are the spirits called up by the control spirit *ob.*

The Hebrew, however, does not only imply that an *ob* is a control spirit, but that it may also be a man or a woman (Lev. 20:27). A person who has a controlling spirit becomes a control spirit—a medium. Most modern-day mediums appear to have one or two controlling spirits in tow. Mediums open themselves up to being channels for communication with the spirits of darkness. The punishment for mediums in the Old Testament was death.

Although the New Testament does modify some of the social and food regulations of the Old Testament, it never withdraws the ban on contact with spirits. On the positive side the New Testament encourages Christians to build up a relationship with God the Father through Jesus Christ.

The spirits of darkness (demons) are unclean, and it is noticeable that those who communicate with them very quickly get led into acts of impurity and will soon lead others into the ways of uncleanness. The Holy Spirit of God is purity and light and enjoins the followers of Jesus Christ to be holy and to walk in the light.

It is then a perfectly proper concern for the church today to be wary, lest in any desire to be open to revelations from God we overlook the clear warnings given concerning all the pagan practices plainly forbidden in the Bible.

Detestable Practices

We have been at pains positively to encourage the operation of the proper revelatory gifts of the Spirit which are holy and supernatural in origin, but there is a basic list of abominable pagan practices which is derived from the occult, a satanic counterfeit of God's true supernatural power.

This manifests itself in three areas: miracles, communication, and knowledge of the future.

Such practice is forbidden because

- It places a person under the control of a power which is not God's—a power which is hostile to the Lord (1 Cor. 10:19–21).
- The lust for certain knowledge which was forbidden to man-

kind was the cause of man's fall. It is portrayed as an attempt to bypass God's specifically stated boundaries (Gen. 3:3–5).

- The desire for such power to spiritually dominate and control others is opposed to God's will (Exod. 3:7–9; Isa. 47:12–15; Micah 6:8).
- It creates a dangerous and destructive personality (Mark 3:27; 5:1–20).
- It is rank disobedience to God; this is rebellion and arrogance (1 Sam. 15:23).
- This road tends to lead downhill into increasingly unclean, degenerating, and destructive practices.

Solemn Warnings

Solemn warnings were repeatedly given to God's chosen people who were about to enter the promised land (Deut. 19:9–13). They were to beware the forbidden practices employed by the Canaanite inhabitants, who were being driven out precisely because of such abominations. The list is spelled out as follows:

1. *Februation.* This is the terribly cruel practice of passing offspring of either sex through fire as sacrifices to heathen gods (Deut. 12:31), supposedly to placate a pagan deity for obtaining some favor or averting some calamity.
2. *Divination.* This was the most prevalent of occult activities in ancient heathendom. It has reappeared in every epoch of human history. In nearly every part of the world evangelized by pioneer Christian missionaries there has been opposition from heathen practitioners of divination. The following list will help to identify some techniques for divination though there are many more: arithmancy (from numbers); coffee-ground reading; bird formation in flight; horoscopy (star-reading); geomancy (dot-reading); cartomancy (card-

reading); crystal glass gazing; capromancy (smoke-reading); pyromancy (fire-reading); tephromancy (ash-reading); tea-leaf-reading in cups; radaesthenia; pendulums; white-of-egg reading in wineglasses.

3. *Sorcery.* The securing of a desired answer by tampering or introducing secret influences (magic) to operate in one's favor.

4. *Soothsaying.* This is especially linked with divination. Both are arts for the unlawful acquisition of knowledge of the future. There is an alternative translation for Numbers 23:23, which is very pertinent. It runs: "There is no omen in Jacob and no divination in Israel. At the appropriate time in Jacob and Israel God gives the revelation." *Whenever it is the right time God will speak to his people by the prophets.* The verse makes a clear distinction between the illegitimate acquisition of knowledge from the powers of darkness and the legitimate means for obtaining information from God.

5. *The practice of witchcraft.* Something which is on the increase again in the Western world today.

6. *Spell-casting.* This effected what amounted to curses. Ezekiel refers to certain women who made use of magic wristbands and veils to put death curses on people and to give assurance of personal safety to others (Ezek. 13:17–23).

7. *Mediumistic practices with a control spirit* (already referred to).

8. *Spiritism* (already referred to).

9. *Necromancy* (consulting the dead). A comprehensive term which includes all forms of spiritism and superstition.

Immorality and Idolatry

These detestable practices were associated with gross immorality (Lev. 20) and idolatry (Lev. 26). They were a constant temptation to the people of Israel and only served to prove that the warnings were indeed all too necessary.

Manasseh, King of Judah, is on record as leading Israel into doing more evil than all the nations who had been driven out by the Lord (2 Kings 21:6,9).

The Sentence of Death

The Old Testament solemnly pronounces the death penalty upon those who fall into such heathen rites (Exod. 22:18; Lev. 20:6, 20, 27; Deut. 17:5). Any Christian believer today who seeks to be open to revelations of the spirit from the Lord God almighty must certainly renounce every such practice which can only lead to defilement, abomination, and ultimate destruction for himself and all who follow him.

DISCERNING PROPHECIES

There is one vital area, which may appear to have been assumed, but it is worth spelling out in an abbreviated form here, although I have dealt with it already more amply at the end of my book, *Does God Speak Today?* (Hodder & Stoughton, 1989).

Let us never overlook the warning of Jesus, who said that in the latter days there would be an attempt to deceive even the elect—if that were possible (Matt. 24:24). Obviously, having prayed for wisdom, we should seek to weigh (1 Cor. 14:29) and to test (1 John 4:1) all prophecies and the spirit behind them.

There are seven obvious tests (1 Thess. 5:21 and 1 John 4:1)·

1. *The prophecy and Scripture.* A vital test is to check how the prophecy squares with the written Word of God, which must be our touchstone (2 Tim. 3:16). There must be no adulteration of Scripture by adding to it anything clearly contrary to God's Word in the Bible. Neither can there be any subtraction from Scripture (Rev. 22:18, 19). No prophecy should be countenanced that contains slander (Ti-

162

tus 3:2). All prophecy must be weighed (1 Cor. 14:29) and tested (1 John 4:1). It is important here to specify that because some aspect of a prophecy or manner of prophesying may not be found literally in the Scriptures, it is not thereby necessarily unscriptural. There are many things we accept as wholesome in domestic and church life that may not be referred to in the Bible at all (e.g., public address systems!), but they are in no way contrary to the Word of God as set forth in holy Scripture.

2. *The prophecy and fulfillment.* We must ask such questions as "Will this come to pass?" The problem here may sometimes be that if we wait to see, it may be too late. If the Ninevites had waited for Jonah's prophecy to come to pass, they would have all been dead! But they repented at once, as they were meant to do (Jonah 3:4,5). It is helpful if the prophet has established a track record locally of his earlier prophecies having been fulfilled. One of the features of the prophecies mentioned in this book is that signs were given to accompany the prophecies, which, when fulfilled, gave credence to what was predicted. Perhaps the classic biblical example of this is Isaiah 38:8—though the signs need not normally be quite so astounding!

3. *The prophecy and fruit.* There are certain obvious tests here. Bad fruit has a bad taste. We should "taste and see" whether the prophecy is in line with what God is already clearly blessing. There are, however, exceptions to this. Philip's work was being greatly blessed in Samaria (Acts 8:6), yet the Lord gave him the word to move on (Acts 8:26). The questions could be put another way: Will this really further the work of God? There must be no hint of personal resentment; suspicion of wishful thinking; the semblance of an ego trip as in the case of an immature person craving visibility in the church; nor an attempt to

use the gift for an improper exercise of control. It must be purely and simply for the glory of God alone.

4. *The prophecy and confirmation.* When all is said and done, it would be most unwise to act in more than a tentative way in response to any prophecy without confirmation from some completely independent source. Also the inner witness from one's own spirit and the external witness from the leadership of the church are necessary. It may be, of course, that the prophecy is a totally independent confirmation for someone about something God has already been revealing in several other ways—usually over a period of time. In this latter case, where it is quite obviously God's will, the person should prepare to obey as soon as possible.

5. *The prophecy and authority.* While Scripture shows that prophets who had words from the Lord for those in authority often delivered them boldly (cf. Nathan in Samuel 12:1–14 and Elijah in 1 Kings 21:17–34), nevertheless Scripture is quite specific that the prophetic ministry must be exercised in a fitting and orderly way (1 Cor. 14:40). This means that it must be exercised among God's people in submission to those in authority (Heb. 13:7). God is not disorderly (1 Cor. 14:33), and the spirits of the prophets are subject to their own control (1 Cor. 14:32).

6. *The character of the prophet*—the fruits of his life. Is it glorifying to God (Matt. 7:16)? This is not an absolute test. God specifically pronounced Abraham a prophet (Gen. 20:7) even though he had just blatantly lied about his wife (Gen. 21:2). Balaam had a good prophecy (Num. 24), but he fell into bad ways (Jude 11). The old prophet in 1 Kings 13:14–26 also lied to the man of God from Judah and then prophesied truly. Therefore, this test is not foolproof, and we shall need to use the other tests alongside it.

7. *The spirit of the prophet.* This is a kind of "resonance" test. Sometimes a prophet can sound so right and biblical and yet others receive a jarring in their own spirit when they hear it. This could well be the gift of distinguishing of spirits, which God has sent to our aid. Scripture shows that some prophecy comes from "a lying spirit" (1 Kin. 22:22). Even true prophecy can come from the enemy for his own devious purposes (Acts 16:17,18), just as the devil cites Scripture (Matt. 4:6). Scripture also reveals that some prophecy is false because it comes from the human spirit (1 Kin. 22:15,16). Presumably the "human spirit" could hazard a correct guess, but this should never be encouraged or trusted. Prophecy that truly comes from the Lord (1 Kin. 22:17). If the prophecy appears strange, it is always good to double-check as far as possible whether the originator is involved with the occult.

Apply the tests of 1 John 4:1, using the gift of distinguishings (1 Cor. 12:10). It seems clear that the spirit of true prophecy testifies of Jesus (Rev. 19:10*b*). Paul says that with the gift of prophecy "though I . . . understand all mysteries and all knowledge . . . but have not love, I am nothing" (1 Cor. 13:2).

Jesus warns that in the last days even the elect may be deceived by miracles (Matt. 24:24). With the gracious gifts of the Spirit in operation and all these checks and balances to hand within the body of Christ, we trust that we shall never be deceived. Thanks be to God!

REFERENCES

Henry Chadwick, *The Early Church,* Penguin, 1968.

Arnold Dallimore, *George Whitefield,* London, 1990.

Rex Gardner, *Healing Miracles,* Darton, Longman & Todd, 1986.

Wayne Gruden, "Introducing the Prophetic Ministry," article in special U. K. edition of *Equipping the Saints,* Fall, 1990.

Wayne Gruden, *The Gift of Prophecy,* Kingsway, 1988.

D. E. Harrell, *All Things are Possible,* Indiana University Press, 1975.

Walter J. Hollenweger, *The Pentecostals,* Augsburg Fortress, 1977.

F. J. A. Hort, *The Ante-Nicene Fathers,* 1895. W. B. Eerdmans, 1951.

Kurt Koch, *Christian Counselling and Occultism,* Kregel Publications, Grand Rapids, 1972.

Ronald A. Knox, *Enthusiasm,* N. E. Collins, 1987.

Christian Lalive d'Epinay, *Haven of the Masses,* Lutterworth Press, 1969.

G. H. Lang, *Divine Guidance,* S. L. Hunt, Rushden, Northants, 1947.

Howard Pittman, *Placebo,* published privately by the author (before November 1983).

John Pridmore, *"Miracles: the Mystery and the Meaning,"* *Crusade* magazine, October, 1976.

Grace City Report, special edition, volume 2, number 5, Kansas City, August, 1989.

References

John and Paula Sandford, *The Elijah Task,* Logos International, Plain-
fields, 1977.

Keith Thomas, *Religion and the Decline of Magic,* Penguin, 1973.

John Wimber, *Equipping the Saints,* Vineyard Ministries International,
Fall, 1989.

J. Stafford Wright, *Christianity and the Occult,* Scripture Union, London, 1971.